Human Rights
in
Cultural & Religious Perspective

Human Rights in Cultural & Religious Perspective

Sarat C. Joshi

AKANSHA PUBLISHING HOUSE
NEW DELHI • GUWAHATI • VISAKHAPATNAM

AKANSHA PUBLISHING HOUSE
4649-B/21, Ansari Road
Darya Ganj, New Delhi - 110 002
Ph.: 23263193 / 9811582579 / 09435116718
Fax: 011-23263193
Email: ektabooks@yahoo.com
www.akanshapublishinghouse.com

Human Rights in Cultural & Religious Perspective

First Published 2010
ISBN 978-81-8370-215-7

PRINTED IN INDIA

Published by Akansha Publishing House, New Delhi and Printed at S.N. Printers, Delhi.

Contents

Preface

> "Some one labeled it `the centruy of the common man', but how much better if we could truthfully label it `the century of the brotherhood of man'."
>
> —*Walter Kiernan*

Basically, `culture' and `religion' are the two important terms of sociology. Here we will take them in the context of basic human rights.

Traditional culture is not a substitute for human rights; it is a cultural context in which human rights must be established, integrated, promoted and protected. Human rights must be approached in a way that is meaningful and relevant in diverse cultural contexts. Rather than limit human rights to suit a given culture, why not draw on traditional cultural values to reinforce the application and relevance of universal human rights? There is an increased need to emphasize the common, core values shared by all cultures: the value of life, social order and protection from arbitrary rule. These basic values are embodied in human rights.

In fact, traditional cultures should be approached and recognized as partners to promote greater respect for and observance of human rights. Drawing on compatible practices and common values from traditional cultures would enhance and advance human rights promotion and protection. This approach not only encourages greater tolerance, mutual respect and understanding, but also fosters more effective international cooperation for human rights.

Greater understanding of the ways in which traditional cultures protect the well-being of their people would illuminate the common foundation of human dignity on which human rights promotion and protection stand. This insight would enable human rights advocacy to assert the cultural relevance, as well as the legal obligation, of universal human rights in 'diverse cultural contexts.

In fact, some modern national constitutions are based on the trinity of liberty, equality and fraternity. In capitalist individualist traditions liberty gets emphasized at the expense of the others; in socialist experiments equality is accepted while liberty and fraternity are sacrificed. In framing the Indian Constitution, Dr. B.R. Ambedkar sought to hold the three together in dynamic unity, in a perichoresis. But now with India's massive surrender to the free market, equality and fraternity have once again fallen victim to the liberty of the wealthy. Profound human rights violations are involved in this process. All these factors constituting human rights point to and lead to and express what they ultimately derive from, namely, human dignity.

Recognition and appreciation of particular cultural contexts would serve to facilitate, rather than reduce, human rights respect and observance. Working in this way with particular cultures inherently recognizes cultural integrity and diversity, without compromising or diluting the unquestionably universal standard of human rights. Such an approach is essential to ensure that the future will be guided above all by human rights, non-discrimination, tolerance and cultural pluralism.

As is obvious from the name of title, the present work

is an attempt to portray a vivid and authentic account of Human rights in cultural and religious perspective. The main topics included herein are:—Introduction; Multiculturalism and Relevent Issues; Human Rights and World Culture; Sociological Route to Human Rights; Natural Law and Natural Rights; and Human Rights from Religious le; and Bibliography etc.

No doubt, the authoritative information will delight and enlighten students, researchers, policy planners, administrators besides social and human rights activists, NGOs and general readers.

With the sole aim for furnishing authoritative information, I have subscribed the views of different scholars in the field of sociology and human rights. As such sources of information are secondary i.e. published articles, books, magazines etc. available in print form or digitally. I am deeply beholden to all those scholars as well as the sources for benefiting from their works. My seniors, colleagues and friends have generously helped, inspired and guided me in my academic pursuits. I am grateful to them all.

I am thankful to my publishers for envincing keen interest in the present venture and materialising this in the present shape that too within shortest possible time.

I will be grateful if the learned readers could send their comments and suggestions for enhancing the quality of information contained in the present volume.

—**SCJ**

1

Introduction

> "Culture is not just an ornament; it is the expression of a nation's character, and at the same time it is a powerful instrument to mould character. The end of culture is right living."
>
> —*W. Somerset Maugham*

Since present work intends to study human rights from cultural and religious view points, it is necessary for every curious reader to know culture thoroughly. In this chapter, first we have made an attempt to portray a vivid accounts of culture.

What is Culture?

In fact, Culture is a term that has different meanings. For example, in 1952, Alfred Kroeber and Clyde Kluckhohn compiled a list of 164 definitions of "culture" in *Culture: A Critical Review of Concepts and Definitions*. However, the word "culture" is most commonly used in three basic senses which are as follows:

1. Excellence of taste in the fine arts and humanities, also known as high culture;
2. An integrated pattern of human knowledge, belief, and behavior that depends upon the capacity for symbolic thought and social learning;

3. The set of shared attitudes, values, goals, and practices that characterizes an institution, organization or group.

When the concept first emerged in eighteenth- and nineteenth-century Europe, it connoted a process of cultivation or improvement, as in agriculture or horticulture. In the nineteenth century, it came to refer first to the betterment or refinement of the individual, especially through education, and then to the fulfillment of national aspirations or ideals. In the mid-nineteenth century, some scientists used the term "culture" to refer to a universal human capacity.

Further in the twentieth century, "culture" emerged as a concept central to anthropology, encompassing all human phenomena that are not purely results of human genetics. Specifically, the term "culture" in American anthropology had two meanings: (a) the evolved human capacity to classify and represent experiences with symbols, and to act imaginatively and creatively; and (b) the distinct ways that people living in different parts of the world classified and represented their experiences, and acted creatively. Following World War II, the term became important, albeit with different meanings, in other disciplines such as sociology, cultural studies, organizational psychology and management studies etc.

In the nineteenth century, humanists such as English poet and essayist Matthew Arnold (1822-1888) used the word "culture" to refer to an ideal of individual human refinement, of "the best that has been thought and said in the world." This concept of culture is comparable to the German concept of *bildung*: "...culture being a pursuit of our total perfection by means of getting to know, on all the matters which most concern us, the best which has been thought and said in the world."

Practically, *culture* referred to an élite ideal and was associated with such activities as art, classical music, and haute cuisine. As these forms were associated with urbane life, "culture" was identified with "civilization" (from lat. *civitas*, city). Another facet of the Romantic movement was an interest in folklore, which led to identifying a "culture" among non-elites. This distinction is often characterized as that between "high culture", namely that of the ruling social group, and "low culture." In other words, the idea of "culture" that developed in Europe during the 18th and early 19th centuries reflected inequalities within European societies. Matthew Arnold contrasted "culture" with "anarchy;" other Europeans, following philosophers Thomas Hobbes and Jean-Jacques Rousseau, contrasted "culture" with "the state of nature."

According to Hobbes and Rousseau, the Native Americans who were being conquered by Europeans from the 16th centuries on were living in a state of nature; this opposition was expressed through the contrast between "civilized" and "uncivilized." According to this way of thinking, one could classify some countries and nations as more civilized than others and some people as more cultured than others. This contrast led to Herbert Spencer's theory of Social Darwinism and Lewis Henry Morgan's theory of cultural evolution.

Just as some critics have argued that the distinction between high and low cultures is really an expression of the conflict between European elites and non-elites, some critics have argued that the distinction between civilized and uncivilized people is really an expression of the conflict between European colonial powers and their colonial subjects. Other 19th century critics, following Rousseau, have accepted this differentiation between higher and lower culture, but have seen the refinement and sophistication of high culture as corrupting and unnatural developments that obscure and distort people's essential nature. These critics considered folk music (as produced by working-class people) to honestly express a natural way of life, while classical music seemed superficial and decadent.

Equally, this view often portrayed indigenous peoples as "noble savages" living authentic and unblemished lives, uncomplicated and uncorrupted by the highly stratified capitalist systems of the West. In 1870 Edward Tylor (1832-1917) applied these ideas of higher versus lower culture to propose a theory of the evolution of religion. According to this theory, religion evolves from more polytheistic to more monotheistic forms. In the process, he redefined culture as a diverse set of activities characteristic of all human societies. This view paved the way for the modern understanding of culture.

The noted philosopher Immanuel Kant (1724–1804) formulated an individualist definition of "enlightenment" similar to the concept of *bildung*: "Enlightenment is man's emergence from his self-incurred immaturity." He argued that this immaturity comes not from a lack of understanding, but from a lack of courage to think independently. Against this intellectual cowardice, Kant urged: *Sapere aude*, "Dare to be wise!" In reaction to Kant, German scholars such as Johann Gottfried Herder (1744–1803) argued that human creativity, which necessarily takes unpredictable and highly diverse forms, is as important as human rationality.

Moreover, Herder proposed a collective form of *bildung*: "For Herder, Bildung was the totality of experiences that provide a coherent identity, and sense of common destiny, to a people." In 1795, the great linguist and philosopher Wilhelm von Humboldt (1767-1835) called for an anthropology that would synthesize Kant's and Herder's interests. During the Romantic era, scholars in Germany, especially those concerned with nationalist movements—such as the nationalist struggle to create a "Germany" out of diverse principalities, and the nationalist struggles by ethnic minorities against the Austro-Hungarian Empire—developed a more inclusive notion of culture as "worldview." According to this school of thought, each ethnic group has a distinct worldview that is incommensurable with the worldviews of other groups. Although more inclusive than earlier views, this approach to culture still allowed for distinctions between "civilized" and "primitive" or "tribal" cultures. In 1860, Adolf Bastian (1826–1905) argued for "the psychic unity of mankind". He proposed that a scientific comparison of all human societies would reveal that distinct worldviews consisted of the same basic elements. According to Bastian, all human societies share a set of "elementary ideas" (*Elementargedanken*); different cultures, or different "folk ideas" (*Volkergedanken*), are local modifications of the elementary ideas. This view paved the way for the modern understanding of culture.

Although anthropologists worldwide refer to Tylor's definition of culture, in the 20th century "culture" emerged as the central and unifying concept of American anthropology, where it most commonly refers to the universal human capacity to classify and encode their experiences symbolically, and communicate symbolically encoded experiences socially. American anthropology is organized into four fields, each of which plays an important role in research on culture: biological anthropology, linguistics, cultural anthropology and archeology. Research in these fields have influenced anthropologists working in other countries to different degrees.

Again, discussion concerning culture among biological anthropologists centers around two debates. First, is culture uniquely human or shared by other species (most notably, other primates)? This is an important question, as the theory of evolution holds that humans are descended from (now extinct) non-human primates. Second, how did culture evolve among human beings? Gerald Weiss noted that although Tylor's classic definition of culture was restricted to humans, many anthropologists take this for granted and thus elide that important qualification from later definitions, merely equating culture with any learned behavior.

This slippage is a problem because during the formative years of modern primatology, some primatologists were trained in anthropology (and understood that culture refers to learned behavior among humans), and others were not. Notable non-anthropologists, like Robert Yerkes and Jane Goodall thus argued that since chimpanzees have learned behaviors, they have culture.

Today, anthropological primatologists are divided, several arguing that non-human primates have culture, others arguing that they do not. This scientific debate is complicated by ethical concerns. The subjects of primatology are non-human primates, and whatever culture these primates have is threatened by human activity.

After reviewing the research on primate culture, W.C. McGrew concluded, "[a] discipline requires subjects, and most species of nonhuman primates are endangered by their human cousins. Ultimately, whatever its merit, cultural primatology must be committed to cultural survival [i.e. to the survival of primate cultures]."

McGrew suggests a definition of culture that he finds

scientifically useful for studying primate culture. He points out that scientists do not have access to the subjective thoughts or knowledge of non-human primates. Thus, if culture is defined in terms of knowledge, then scientists are severely limited in their attempts to study primate culture. Instead of defining culture as a kind of knowledge, McGrew suggests that we view culture as a process. He lists six steps in the process:

1. A new pattern of behavior is invented, or an existing one is modified.
2. The innovator transmits this pattern to another.
3. The form of the pattern is consistent within and across performers, perhaps even in terms of recognizable stylistic features.
4. The one who acquires the pattern retains the ability to perform it long after having acquired it.
5. The pattern spreads across social units in a population. These social units may be families, clans, troops, or bands.
6. The pattern endures across generations.

Obviously, McGrew admits that all six criteria may be strict, given the difficulties in observing primate behavior in the wild. But he also insists on the need to be as inclusive as possible, on the need for a definition of culture that "casts the net widely": Culture is considered to be group-specific behavior that is acquired, at least in part, from social influences. Here, group is considered to be the species-typical unit, whether it be a troop, lineage, subgroup, or so on. *Prima facia* evidence of culture comes from within-species but across-group variation in behavior, as when a pattern is persistent in one community of chimpanzees but is absent from another, or when different communities perform different versions of the same pattern. The suggestion of culture in action is stronger when the difference across the groups cannot be explained solely by ecological factors ....

Charles Frederick Voegelin pointed out, if "culture" is reduced to "learned behavior," then all animals have culture. Certainly all specialists agree that all primate species evidence common cognitive skills: knowledge of object-permanence, cognitive mapping, the ability to categorize objects, and creative problem solving.

Moreover, all primate species show evidence of shared social skills: they recognize members of their social group; they form direct relationships based on degrees of kinship and rank; they recognize third-party social relationships; they predict future behavior; and they cooperate in problem-solving. Nevertheless, the term "culture" applies to non-human animals only if we define culture as any or all learned behavior. Within mainstream physical anthropology, scholars tend to think that a more restrictive definition is necessary. These researchers are concerned with how human beings evolved to be different from other species.

A more precise definition of culture, which excludes non-human social behavior, would allow physical anthropologists to study how humans evolved their unique capacity for "culture". Chimpanzees (*Pan troglodytes* and *Pan paniscus*) are humans' (*Homo sapiens*) closest living relative; both are descended from a common ancestor which lived around five or six million years ago.

This is the same amount of time it took for horses and zebras, lions and tigers, and rats and mice, to diverge from their respective common ancestors The evolution of modern humans is rapid: *Australopithicenes* evolved four million years ago and modern humans in past several hundred thousand years. During this time humanity evolved three distinctive features:

(a) the creation and use of conventional symbols, including linguistic symbols and their derivatives, such as written language and mathematical symbols and notations;
(b) the creation and use of complex tools and other instrumental technologies; and
(c) the creation and participation in complex social organization and institutions.

According to Michael Tomasello, "where these complex and species-unique behavioral practices, and the cognitive skills that underlie them, came from" is a fundamental anthropological question. Given that contemporary humans and chimpanzees are far more different than horses and zebras, or rats and mice, and that the evolution of this great difference occurred in such a short period of time, "our search must be for some small difference that made a big difference – some adaptation, or small set of adaptations, that changed the process of primate cognitive evolution in fundamental ways." According to Tomasello, the answer to this question must form the basis of a scientific definition of "human culture."

In a recent review of the major research on human and primate tool-use, communication, and learning strategies, Tomasello argues that the key human advances over primates (language, complex technologies, complex social organization) are all the results of humans pooling cognitive resources.

This is called "the ratchet effect:" innovations spread and are shared by a group, and mastered "by youngsters, which enables them to remain in their new and improved form within the group until something better comes along." The key point is that children are born good at a particular kind of social learning; this creates a favored environment for social innovations, making them more likely to be maintained and transmitted to new generations than individual innovations.

For Tomasello, human social learning—the kind of learning that distinguishes humans from other primates and that played a decisive role in human evolution—is based on two elements: first, what he calls "imitative learning," (as opposed to "emulative learning" characteristic of other primates) and second, the fact that humans represent their experiences symbolically (rather than iconically, as is characteristic of other primates). Together, these elements enable humans to be both inventive, and to preserve useful inventions. It is this combination that produces the ratchet effect.

The kind of learning found among other primates is "emuluation learning," which "focuses on the environmental events involved – results or changes of state in the environment that the other produced – rather than on the actions that produced those results." Tomasello emphasizes that emulation learning is a highly adaptive strategy for apes because it focuses on the effects of an act. In laboratory experiments, chimpanzees were shown two different ways for using a rake-like tool to obtain an out-of-reach-object. Both methods were effective, but one was more efficient than the other. Chimpanzees consistently emulated the more efficient method.

The kind of learning characteristic of human children is "Imitative learning," which "means reproducing an instrumental act understood intentionally." Human infants begin to display some evidence of this form of learning between the ages of nine and twelve months, when infants fix their attention not only on an object, but on the gaze of an adult which enables them to use adults as points of reference and thus "act on objects in the way adults are acting on them."

This dynamic is well-documented and has also been termed "joint engagement" or "joint attention." Essential to this dynamic is the infants growing capacity to recognize others as "intentional agents:" people "with the power to control their spontaneous behavior" and who "have goals and make active choices among behavioral means for attaining those goals." The development of skills in joint attention by the end of a human child's first year of life provides the basis for the development of imitative learning in the second year. In one study 14-month old children imitated an adult's overly-complex method of turning on a light, even when they could have used an easier and more natural motion to the same effect. In another study, 16-month old children interacted with adults who alternated between a complex series of motions that appeared intentional and a comparable set of motions that appeared accidental; they imitated only those motions that appeared intentional. Another study of 18-month old children revealed that children imitate actions that adults intend , yet in some way fail, to perform. Tomasello emphasizes that this kind of imitative learning "relies fundamentally on infants' tendency to identify with adults, and on their ability to distinguish in the actions of others the underlying goal and the different means that might be used to achieve it."

He calls this kind of imitative learning “cultural learning because the child is not just learning about things from other persons, she is also learning things through them — in the sense that she must know something of the adult’s perspective on a situation to learn the active use of this same intentional act.” He concludes that the key feature of cultural learning is that it occurs only when an individual “understands others as intentional agents, like the self, who have a perspective on the world that can be followed into, directed and shared”

Tomasello further argues that cultural learning is essential for language-acquisition. Most children in any society, and all children in some, do not learn all words through the direct efforts of adults. “In general, for the vast majority of words in their language, children must find a way to learn in the ongoing flow of social interaction, sometimes from speech not even addressed to them.” This finding has been confirmed by a variety of experiments in which children learned words even when the referent was not present, multiple referents were possible, and the adult was not directly trying to teach the word to the child.

Tomasello concludes that “a linguistic symbol is nothing other than a marker for an intersubjectively shared understanding of a situation. Tomasello’s 1999 review of the research contrasting human and non-human primate learning strategies confirms biological anthropologist Ralph Holloway’s 1969 argument that a specific kind of sociality linked to symbolic cognition were the keys to human evolution, and constitute the nature of culture.

According to Holloway, the key issue in the evolution of *H. sapiens*, and the key to understanding “culture,” “is how man organizes his experience.” Culture is “the *imposition of arbitrary form upon the environment.*" This fact, Holloway argued, is primary to and explains what is distinctive about human learning strategies, tool-use, and language. Human tool-making and language express "similar, if not identical, cognitive processes" and provide important evidence for how humankind evolved. In other words, whereas McGrew argues that anthropologists must focus on behaviors like communication and tool-use because they have no access to the mind, Holloway argues that human language and tool-use, including the earliest stone tools in the fossil record, are highly suggestive of cognitive differences between humans and non-humans, and that such cognitive differences in turn explain human evolution.

For Holloway, the question is not whether other primates communicate, learn or make tools, but that the *way* they do these things. "Washing potatoes in the ocean ... stripping branches of leaves to get termites," and other examples of primate tool-use and learning "are iconic, and there is no feedback from the environment to the animal ." Human tools, however, express an independence from natural form that manifests symbolic thinking. "In the preparation of the stick for termite-eating, the relation between product and raw material is iconic. In the making of a stone tool, in contrast, there is no necessary relation between the form of the final product and the original material."

In Holloway's view, our non-human ancestors, like those of modern chimpanzees and other primates, shared motor and sensory skills, curiosity, memory, and intelligence, with perhaps differences in degree. "It is when these are integrated with the unique attributes of arbitrary production (symbolization) and imposition that man qua cultural man appears."

Linguists Charles Hockett and R. Ascher have identified thirten design-features of language, some shared by other forms of animal connunication. One feature that distinguishes human language is its tremendous productivity; in other words, competent speakers of a language are capable of producing an infinite number of original utterances.

This productivity seems to be made possible by a few critical features unique to human language. One is "duality of patterning," meaning that human language consists of the articulation of several distinct processes, each with its own set of rules: combining phonemes to produce morphemes, combining morphemes to produce words, and combining words to produce sentences. This means that a person can master a relatively limited numper of signals and sets of rules, to create infinite combinations.

Another crucial element is that human language is symbolic: the sound of words (or their shape, when written) bear no relation to what they represent. In other words, their meaning is arbitrary. That words have meaning is a matter of convention. Since the meaning of words are arbitrary, any word may have several meanings, and any object may be referred to using a variety of words; the actual word used to describe a particular object depends on the context, the intention of the speaker, and the ability of the listener to judge these appropriately. As Tomasello notes. An individual language user looks at a tree and, before drawing the attention of her interlocutor to that tree, must decide, based on her assessment of the listener's current knowledge and expectations, whether to say "that tree over there," "it," "the oak," "that hundred-year-oak," "the tree," "the bagswing tree," "that thing in the front yard," "the ornament," "the embarrassment," or any of a number of other expressions. ... And these decisions are not made on the basis of the speaker's direct goal with respect to the object or activity involved, but rather that they are made on the basis of her goal with respect to the listener's interest and attention to that object or activity.

Returning to matter of syntax, rules, and concatenated activity mentioned above, almost any model which describes a language process can also be used to describe tool-making. This is hardly surprising. Both activities are concatenated, both have rigid rules about eh serialization of unit activities (the grammar, syntax), both are hierarchical systems of activity (as is any motor activity), and both produce arbitrary configurations which thence become part of the environment, either temporarily or permanently.

Productivity can be seen in the facts that basic types were probably used for multiple purposes, that tool industries tend to expand with time, and that a slight variation on h basic pattern may be made to met some new functional requisite. Elements of a basic "vocabulary" of motor operations—flakes, detachment, rotation, preparation of striking platform, etc.—are used in different combinations to produce dissimilar tools, with different forms, and supposedly, different uses. . . . Taking each motor event alone, no one action is complete; each action depends on the prior one and requires a further one, and each is dependent in another ay on the original plan. In other words, at each point of the action except the last, the piece is not "satisfactory" in structure. Each unit action is meaningless by itself in the sense of the use of the tool; it is meaningful only in the context of the whole completed set of actions culminating in the final product. This exactly parallels language.

As Tomasello has demonstrated, symbolic thought can operate only in a particular social environment:

> Arbitrary symbols enforce consensus of perceptions, which not only allows members to communicate about the same objects in terms of space and time (as in hunting) but it also makes it possible for social relationships to be standardized and manipulated through symbols. It means that idiosyncracies are smoothed out and perceived within classes of behavior. By enforcing perceptual invariance, symbols also enforce social behavioral constancy, and enforcing social behavioral constancy is a prerequisite to differential task-role sectors in a differentiated social group adapting not only to the outside environment but to its own membership.

> Once some useful behavior spreads within a population and becomes more important for subsistence, it will generate selection pressures on genetic traits that support its propagation ... Stone and tymbolic tools, which were initially acquired with the aid of flexible ape-learning abilities, ultimately turned the tables on their users and forced them to adapt to a new niche opened by these technologies. Rather than being just useful tricks, these behavioral proshteses for obtaining food and organizing social behaviors became indispensible elements in a new adaptive complex. The origin of "humanness" can be defined as that point in our evolution where these tools became the principle source of selection on our bodies and brains. It is the diagnostic of *Homo symbolicus*.

Deacon is of the opinion that this occurred between 2 and 2.5 million years ago, when we have the first fossil evidence of stone tool use and the beginning of a trend in an increase in brain size. But it is the evolution of symbolic language which is the cause—and not the effect—of these trends. More specifically, Deacon is suggesting that *Australopithecines*, like contemporary apes, used tools; it is possible that over the millions of years of *Australopithecine* history, many troops developed symbolic communication systems. All that was necessary was that one of these groups so altered their environment that "it introduced selection for very different learning abilities than affected prior species."

This troop or population kick-started the Baldwinian process (the "ratchet effect") that led to their evolution to genus *Homo*. The question for Deacon is, what behavioral-environmental changes could have made the development of symbolic thinking adaptive? Here he emphasizes the importance of distinguishing hmans from all other species, not in order to privilege human intelligence but to problematize it. Given that the evolution of *H. sapiens* began with ancestors who did not yet have "culture," what led them to move away from cognitive, learning, communication, and tool-making strategies that were and continued to be adaptive for most other primates (and, some have suggested, most other species of animals)?

Learning symbol systems is more time consuming than other forms of communication, so symbolic thought made possible a different communication strategy, but not a more efficient one than other primates. Nevertheless, it must have offered some selective advantage of *H. sapiens* to have evolved. Deacon starts by looking a two key determinents in evolutionary history: foraging behavior, and patterns of sexual relations.

As he observes competition for sexual access limits the possibilities for social cooperation in many species; yet,

Deacon observes, there are three consistent patterns in human reproduction that distinguish them from other species:

1. Both males and females usually contribute effort towards the rearing of their offspring, though often to differing extents and in very different ways.
2. In all societies, the great majority if adult males and females are bound by long-term, exlusive secual access rights and pronibitions to particular individuals of the opposite sex.
3. They maintain these exclusive sexual relations while living in modest to large-sized, multi-male, multi-female, cooperative social groups.

Moreover, there is one feature common to all known human foraging societies, and markedly different from other primates: "the use of meat. . . . The appearance of the first stone tools nearly 2.5 million years ago almost certainly correlates with a radical shift in foraging behavior in order to gain access to meat."

Deacon does not believe that symbolic thought was necessary for hunting or tool-making (although tool-making may be a reliable index of symbolic thought); rather, it was necessary for the success of distinctive social relations. The key is that while men and women are equally effective foragers, mothers carrying dependent children are not effective hunters. They must thus depend on male hunters. This favors a system in which males have exclusive sexual access to females, and females can predict that their sexual partner will provide food for them and their children.

Human reliance on resources that are relatively unavailable to females with infants selects not only for coopartion between a child's father and mother but also for the cooperation of other relatives and friends, including elderly individuals and juveniles, who can be relied upon for assistance. The special demands of acquiring meat and caring for infants in our own evolution together contribute to the underlying impetus for the third characteristic feature of human reproductive patterns: cooperative group living. What is uniquely characteristic about human societies is what required symbolic cognition, which consequently leads to the evolution of culture: "cooperative, mixed-sex social groups, with significant male care and provisioning of offspring, and relatively stable patterns of reproductive exclusion."

This combination is relatively rare in other species because it is "highly susceptible to disintegration." Language and culture provide the glue that holds it together.

The first forms of symbolic thinking made stone-tools possible, which in turn made hunting for meat a more dependable source of food for our nonhuman ancestors while making possible forms of social communication that make sharing—between males and females, but also among males, decreasing sexual competition: So the socio-ecological problem posed by the transition to a meat-supplemented subsistence strategy is that it cannot be utilized without a social structure which guarantees unambiguous and exclusive mating and is sufficiently egalitarian to sustain cooperation via shared or parallel reproductive interests. This problem can be solved symbolically. Symbols and symbolic thinking thus make possible a central feature of social relations in every human population: reciprocity.

Evolutionary scientists have developed a model to explain reciprocal altruism among closely related individuals. Symbolic thought makes possible reciprocity between distantly related individuals.

Now we come to archeological approaches to culture. In the 19th century archeology was often a supplement to history, and the goal of archeologists was to identify artifacts according to their typology and stratigraphy, thus marking their location in time and space. Franz Boas established that archeology be one of American anthropology's four fields, and debates among archeologists have often paralleled debates among cultural anthropologists. In the 1920s and 1930s, Australian-British archeologist V. Gordon Childe and American archeologist W. C. McKern independently began moving from asking about the date of an artifact, to asking about the people who produced it — when archeologists work alongside historians, historical materials generally help answer these questions, but when historical materials are unavailable, archeologists had to develop new methods. Childe and McKern focused on analyzing the relationships among objects found together.

Childe argued that a "constantly recurring assemblage of artifacts" to be an "archaeological culture." Childe and others viewed "each archeological culture ... the manifestation in material terms of a specific *people*." In 1948 Walter Taylor systematized the methods and concepts that archeologists had developed and proposed a general model for the archeological contribution to knoweldge of cultures. He began with the mainstream understanding of culture as the product of human cognitive activity, and the Boasian emphasis on the subjective meanings of objects as dependent on their cultural context. He defined culture as "a mental phenomenon, consisting of the contents of minds, not of material objects or observable behavior." He then devised a three-tiered model linking cultural anthropology to archeology, which he called conjunctive archeology:

1. Culture, which is unobservable and nonmaterial;
2. Behaviors resulting from culture, which are observable and nonmaterial; and
3. Objectifications, such as artifacts and architecture, which are the result of behavior and material.

That is, material artifacts were the material residue of culture, but not culture itself. Taylor's point was that the archeological record could contribute to anthropological knowledge, but only if archeologists reconceived their work not just as digging up artifacts and recording their location in time and space, but as inferring from material remains the behaviors through which they were produced and used, and inferring from these behaviors the mental activities of people.

Although many archeologists agreed that their research was integral to anthropology, Taylor's program was never fully implemented. One reason was that his three-tier model of inferences required too much fieldwork and laboratory analysis to be practical. Moreover, his view that material remains were not themselves cultural, and in fact twice-removed from culture, in fact left archeology marginal to cultural anthropology.

In 1962 Lewis Binford proposed a new model for anthropological archeology, called "the New Archeology" or "Processual Archeology," based on White's definition of culture as "the extra-somatic means of adaptation for the human organism."

This definition allowed Binford to establish archeology

as a crucial field for the pursuit of the methodology of Julian Steward's cultural ecology: The comparative study of cultural systems with variable technologies in a similar environmental range or similar technologies in differing environments is a major methodology of what Steward has called "cultural ecology," and certainly is a valuable means of increasing our understanding of cultural processes. Such a methodology is also useful in elucidating the structural relationships between major cultural sub-systems such as the social and ideological sub-systems.

In other words, Binford proposed an archeology that would be central to the dominant project of cultural anthropologists at the time (culture as non-genetic adaptations to the environment); the "new archeology" was the cultural anthropology (in the form of cultural ecology or ecological anthropology) of the past.

In the 1980s, there was a movement in the United Kingdom and Europe against the view of archeology as a field of anthropology, echoing Radcliffe-Brown's earlier rejection of cultural anthropology. During this same period, then-Cambridge archeologist Ian Hodder developed "post-processual archeology" as an alternative. Like Binford (and unlike Taylor) Hodder views artifacts not as objectifications of culture but *as* culture itself. Unlike Binford, however, Hodder does not view culture as an environmental adaptation. Instead, he "is committed to a fluid semiotic version of the traditional culture concept in which material items, artifacts, are full participants in the creation, deployment, alteration, and fading away of symbolic complexes."

Language and Culture

It is pertinent to note that connection between culture

and language has been noted as far back as the classical period and probably long before. The ancient Greeks, for example, distinguished between civilized peoples and bárbaros "those who babble", i.e. those who speak unintelligible languages. The fact that different groups speak different, unintelligible languages is often considered more tangible evidence for cultural differences than other less obvious cultural traits. The German romanticists of the 19th century such as Herder, Wundt and Humbolt, often saw language not just as one cultural trait among many but rather as the direct expression of a people's national character, and as such as culture in a kind of condensed form.

Franz Boas, like his German forerunners, maintained that the shared language of a community is the most essential carrier of their common culture. Boas was the first anthropologist who considered it unimaginable to study the culture of a foreign people without also becoming acquainted with their language. For Boas, the fact that the intellectual culture of a people was largely constructed, shared and maintained through the use of language, meant that understanding the language of a cultural group was the key to understanding its culture. At the same time, though, Boas and his students were aware that culture and language are not directly dependent on one another.

That is, groups with widely different cultures may share a common language, and speakers of completely unrelated languages may share the same fundamental cultural traits. Numerous other scholars have suggested that the form of language determines specific cultural traits. This is similar to the notion of Linguistic determinism, which states that the form of language determines individual thought. While Boas himself rejected a causal link between language and culture, some of his intellectual heirs entertained the idea that habitual patterns of speaking and thinking in a particular language may influence the culture of the linguistic group. Such belief is related to the theory of Linguistic relativity.

No doubt, the origin of language, understood as the human capacity of complex symbolic communication, and the origin of complex culture is often thought to stem from the same evolutionary process in early man. Linguists and evolutionary anthropologists suppose that language evolved as early humans began to live in large communities which required the use of complex communication to maintain social coherence. Language and culture then both emerged as a means of using symbols to construct social identity and maintain coherence within a social group too large to rely exclusively on pre-human ways of building community such as for example grooming. Since language and culture are both in essence symbolic systems, twentieth century cultural theorists have applied the methods of analyzing language developed in the science of linguistics to also analyze culture.

Particularly the structural theory of Ferdinand de Saussure, which describes symbolic systems as consisting of signs (a pairing of a particular form with a particular meaning), has come to be applied widely in the study of culture. But also post-structuralist theories, that nonetheless still rely on the parallel between language and culture as systems of symbolic communication, have been applied in the field of semiotics. The parallel between language and culture can then be understood as analog to the parallel between a linguistic sign, consisting for example of the sound [kau] and the meaning "cow", and a cultural sign, consisting for example of the cultural form of "wearing a crown" and the cultural meaning of "being king". In this way it can be argued that culture is itself a kind of language.

Another parallel between cultural and linguistic systems is that they are both systems of practice, that is they are a set of special ways of doing things that is constructed and perpetuated through social interactions. Children, for example, acquire language in the same way as they acquire the basic cultural norms of the society they grow up in - through interaction with older members of their cultural group. However, languages, now understood as the particular set of speech norms of a particular community, are also a part of the larger culture of the community that speak them. Humans use language as a way of signalling identity with one cultural group and difference from others.

Even among speakers of one language several different ways of using the language exist, and each is used to signal affiliation with particular subgroups within a larger culture. In linguistics such different ways of using the same language are called "varities". For example, the English language is spoken differently in the USA, the UK and Australia, and even within English-speaking countries there are hundreds of dialects of English that each signal a belonging to a particular region and/or subculture. For example, in the UK the cockney dialect signals its speakers' belonging to the group of lower class workers of east London. Differences between varieties of the same language often consist in different pronunciations and vocabulary, but also sometimes of different grammatical systems and very often in using different styles (e.g. cockney Rhyming slang or Lawyers' jargon).

Linguists and anthropologists, particularly sociolinguists, ethnolinguists and linguistic anthropologists have specialized in studying how ways of speaking vary between speech communities. A community's ways of speaking or signing are a part of the community's culture, just as other shared practices are. Language use is a way of establishing and displaying group identity. Ways of speaking function not only to facilitate communication, but also to identify the social position of the speaker. Linguists calls different ways of speaking language varieties, a term that encompasses geographically or socioculturally defined dialects as well as the jargons or styles of subcultures. Linguistic anthropologists and sociologists of language define communicative style as the ways that language is used and understood within a particular culture.

The differences between languages does not consist only in differences in pronunciation, vocabulary or grammar, but also in different "cultures of speaking". Some cultures for example have elaborate systems of "social deixis", systems of signalling social distance through linguistic means. In English, social deixis is shown mostly though distinguishing between addressing some people by first name and others by surname, but also in titles such as "Mrs.", "boy", "Doctor" or "Your Honor", but in other languages such systems may be highly complex and codified in the entire grammar and vocabulary of the language. In several languages of east Asia, for example Thai, Burmese and Javanese, different words are used according to whether a speaker is addressing someone of higher or lower rank than one self in a ranking system with animals and children ranking the lowest and gods and membes of royalty as the highest. Other languages may use different forms of address when speaking to speakers of the opposite gender or in-law relatives and many languages have special ways of speaking to infants and children. Among other groups, the culture of speaking may entail *not speaking* to particular people, for example many indigenous cultures of Australia have a taboo against talking to one's in-law relatives, and in some cultures speech is not addressed directly to children.

Now we will discuss. Culture in the purview of cultural anthropology. The modern anthropological understanding of culture has its origins in the 19th century with German anthropologist Adolf Bastian's theory of the "psychic unity of mankind," which, influenced by Herder and von Humboldt, challenged the identification of "culture" with the way of life of European elites, and British anthropologist Edward Burnett Tylor's attempt to define culture as inclusively as possible. Tylor in 1874 described culture in the following way: "Culture or civilization, taken in its wide ethnographic sense, is that complex whole which includes knowledge, belief, art, morals, law, custom, and any other capabilities and habits acquired by man as a member of society." Although Tylor was not aiming to propose a general theory of culture (he explained his understanding of culture in the course of a larger argument about the nature of religion), American anthropologists have generally presented their various definitions of culture as refinements of Tylor's. Franz Boas's student Alfred Kroeber (1876–1970) identified culture with the "superorganic," that is, a domain with ordering principles and laws that could not be explained by or reduced to biology. In 1973, Gerald Weiss reviewed various definitions of culture and debates as to their parsimony and power, and proposed as the most scientifically useful definition that "culture" be defined "as our generic term for all human nongenetic, or metabiological, phenomena".

Franz Boas, founded modern American anthropology with the establishment of the first graduate program in anthropology at Columbia University in 1896. At the time the dominant model of culture was that of cultural evolution, which posited that human societies progressed through stages of savagery to barbarism to civilization; thus, societies that for example are based on horticulture and Iroquois kinship terminology are less evolved that societies based on agriculture and Eskimo kinship terminology.

One of Boas's greatest accomplishments was to demonstrate convincingly that this model is fundamentally flawed, empirically, methodologically, and theoretically. Moreover, he felt that our knowledge of different cultures was so incomplete, and often based on unsystematic or unscientific research, that it was impossible to develop any scientifically valid general model of human cultures. Instead, he established the principle of cultural relativism and trained students to conduct rigorous participant observation field research in different societies. Boas understood the capacity for culture to involve symbolic thought and social learning, and considered the evolution of a capacity for culture to coincide with the evolution of other, biological, features defining genus Homo. Nevertheless, he argued that culture could not be reduced to biology or other expressions of symbolic thought, such as language. Boas and his students understood culture inclusively and resisted developing a general definition of culture. Indeed, they resisted identifying "culture" as a thing, instead using culture as an adjective rather than a noun. Boas argued that cultural "types" or "forms" are always in a state of flux. Alfred Kroeber argued that the "unlimited receptivity and assimilativeness of culture" made it practically impossible to think of cultures as discrete things.

Others, such as Ruth Benedict (1887–1948) and Margaret Mead (1901–1978), produced monographs or comparative studies analyzing the forms of creativity possible to individuals within specific cultural configurations. Essential to their research was the concept of "context": culture provided a context that made the behavior of individuals understandable; geography and history provided a context for understanding the differences between cultures.

Thus, although Boasians were committed to the belief in the psychic unity of humankind and the universality of culture, their emphasis on local context and cultural diversity led them away from proposing cultural universals or universal theories of culture. There is a tension in cultural anthropology between the claim that culture as a universal (the fact that all human societies have culture), and that it is also particular (culture takes a tremendous variety of forms around the world). Since Boas, two debates have dominated cultural anthropology. The first has to do with ways of modeling particular cultures.

Specifically, anthropologists have argued as to whether "culture" can be thought of as a bounded and integrated thing, or as a quality of a diverse collection of things, the numbers and meanings of which are in constant flux. Boas's student Ruth Benedict suggested that in any given society cultural traits may be more or less "integrated," that is, constituting a pattern of action and thought that gives purpose to people's lives, and provides them with a basis from which to evaluate new actions and thoughts, although she implies that there are various degrees of integration; indeed, she observes that some cultures fail to integrate. Boas, however, argued that complete integration is rare and that a given culture only appears to be integrated because of observer bias. For Boas, the appearance of such patterns—a national culture, for example—was the effect of a particular point of view.

"Anthropological work has been overwhelmingly devoted to the analysis of cultural traits," Ruth Benedict "rather than to the study of cultures as articulated wholes." Influenced by Polish-British social anthropologist Bronislaw Malinowski, however, she argued that "The first essential, so it seems today, is to study the living culture, to know its habits of thought and the functions of its institutions" and that "the only way in which we can know the significance of the selected detail of behavior is against the background of the motives and emotions and values that are institutionalized in that culture."

Influenced by German historians Wilhelm Dilthey and Oswald Spengler, as well as by gestalt psychology, she argued that "the whole determines its parts, not only their relation but their very nature," and that "cultures, likewise, are more than the sum of their traits." Just as each spoken language draws very selectively from an extensive, but finite, set of sounds any human mouth (free from defect) can make, she concluded that in each society people, over time and through both conscious and unconscious processes, selected from an extensive but finite set of cultural traits which then combine to form a unique and distinctive pattern." The significance of cultural behavior is not exhausted when we have clearly understood that it is local and man-made and hugely variable. It tends to be integrated. A culture, like an individual, is a more or less consistent pattern of thought and action. Within each culture there come into being characteristic purposes not necessarily shared by other types of society. In obedience to their purposes, each people further and further consolodates its experience, and in proportion to the urgency of these drives the heterogeneous items of behavior take more and more congruous shape.

Taken up by a well-integrated culture, the most ill-assorted acts become characteristic of its particular goals, often by the most unlikely metamorphoses. Although Benedict felt that virtually all cultures are patterened, she argued that these patterns change over time as a consequence of human creativity, and therefore different societies around the world had distinct characters. Benedict observed that many Westerners felt that this view forced them to abandon their "dreams of permanence and ideality and with the individual's illusions of autonomy" and that for many, this made existence "empty." She argued however that once people accepted the results of scientific research, people would "arrive then at a more realistic social faith, accepting as grounds of hope and as new bases for tolerance the coexisting and equally valid patterns of life which mankind has created for itself from the raw materials of existence."

This view of culture has had a tremendous impact outside of anthropology, and dominated American anthropology until the Cold War, when anthropologists like Sidney Mintz and Eric Wolf rejected the validity and value of approaching "each culture" as "a world in itself" and "relatively stable." They felt that, too often, this approach ignored the impact of imperialism, colonialism, and the world capitalist economy on the peoples Benedict and her followers studied (and thus re-opened the debate on the relationship between the universal and the particular, in the form of the relationship between the global and the local). In the meantime, its emphasis on metamorphising patterns influenced French structuralism and made American anthropologists receptive to British structural-functionalism.

Although Boas argued that anthropologists had yet to

collect enough solid evidence from a diverse sample of societies to make any valid general or universal claims about culture, by the 1940s some felt ready. Whereas Kroeber and Benedict had argued that "culture"—which could refer to local, regional, or trans-regional scales—was in some way "patterned" or "configured," some anthropologists now felt that enough data had been collected to demonstrate that it often took highly structured forms. The question these anthropologists debated was, were these structures statistical artifacts, or where they expressions of mental models?

French anthropologist Claude Lévi-Strauss's structuralist anthropology brought together ideas of Boas (especially Boas's belief in the mutability of cultural forms, and Bastian's belief in the psychic unity of humankind) and Émile Durkheim's focus on social structures (institutionalized relationships among persons and groups of persons). Instead of making generalizations that applied to large numbers of societies, Lévi-Strauss sought to derive from concrete cases increasingly abstract models of human nature. His method begins with the supposition that culture exists in two different forms: the many distinct structures that could be inferred from observing members of the same society interact (and of which members of a society are themselves aware), and abstract structures developed by analyzing shared ways (such as myths and rituals) members of a society represent their social life (and of which members of a society are not only *not* consciously aware, and which typically stand in opposition to, or negate, the social structures of which people *are* aware). He then sought to develop one universal mental structure that could only be inferred through the systematic comparison of particular social and cultural structures.

He argued that just as there are laws through which a finite and relatively small number of chemical elements could be combined to create a seemingly infinite variety of things, there were a finite and relatively small number of cultural elements which people combine to create the great variety of cultures anthropologists observe. The systematic comparison of societies would enable an anthropologist to develop this cultural "table of elements," and once completed, this table of cultural elements would enable an anthropologist to analyze specific cultures and achieve insights hidden to the very people who produced and lived through these cultures.

Murdock's HRAF and Lévi-Strauss's structuralism provide two ambitious ways to seek the universal in the particular, and both approaches continue to appeal to different anthropologists. However, the differences between them reveal a tension implicit in the heritage of Tylor and Bastian. Is culture to be found in empirically observed behaviors that may form the basis of generalizations? Or does it consist of universal mental processes, which must be inferred and abstracted from observed behavior? This question has driven debates among biological anthropologists and archeologists as well.

Society Versus Culture

In the 1940s the Boasian understanding of culture was challenged by a new paradigm for anthropological and social science research called Structural functionalism. This paradigm developed independently but in parallel in both the United Kingdom and in the United States. Whereas the Boasians viewed anthropology as that natural science dedicated to the study of humankind, structural functionalists viewed anthropology as one social science among many, dedicated to the study of one specific facet of humanity. This led structural-functionalists to redefine and minimize the scope of "culture."

In the United Kingdom, the creation of structural functionalism was anticipated by Raymond Firth's (1901–2002) *We the Tikopia*, published in 1936, and marked by the publication of *African Political Systems*, edited by Meyer Fortes (1906–1983) and E.E. Evans-Pritchard (1902–1973) in 1940. In these works these anthropologists forwarded a synthesis of the ideas of their mentor, Bronislaw Malinowski (1884-1942), and his rival, A.R. Radcliffe-Brown (1881–1955). Both Malinowski and Radcliffe-Brown viewed anthropology—what they call "social anthropology"—as that branch of sociology that studied so-called primitive societies. According to Malinowski's theory of functionalism, all human beings have certain biological needs, such as the need for food and shelter, and humankind has the biological need to reproduce. Every society develops its own institutions, which function to fulfill these needs. In order for these institutions to function, individuals take on particular social roles that regulate how they act and interact.

Although members of any given society may not understand the ultimate functions of their roles and institutions, an ethnographer can develop a model of these functions through the careful observation of social life. Radcliffe-Brown rejected Malinowski's notion of function, and believed that a general theory of primitive social life could only be built up through the careful comparison of different societies.

Influenced by the work of French sociologist Émile Durkheim (1858–1917), who argued that primitive and modern societies are distinguished by distinct social structures, Radcliffe-Brown argued that anthropologists first had to map out the social structure of any given society before comparing the structures of different societies. Firth, Fortes, and Evans-Pritchard found it easy to combine Malinowski's attention to social roles and institutions with Radcliffe-Brown's concern with social structures. They distinguished between "social organization" (observable social interactions) and "social structure" (rule-governed patterns of social interaction), and shifted their attention from biological functions to social functions (for example, how different institutions are functionally integrated, and the extent to, and ways in, which institutions function to promote social solidarity and stability. In short, instead of culture (understood as all human non-genetic or extra-somatic phenomena)they made "sociality" (interations and relationships among persons and groups of people) their object of study. (Indeed, Radcliffe-Brown once wrote "I should like to invoke a taboo on the word *culture*.")

Remarkably, in 1946 Talcott Parsons founded the Department of Social Relations at Harvard University. Influenced by such European sociologists as Émile Durkheim and Max Weber, Parsons developed a theory of social action that was closer to British social anthropology than to Boas's American anthropology, and which he also called "structural functionalism." Parson's intention was to develop a total theory of social action (why people act as they do), and to develop at Harvard and inter-disciplinary program that would direct research according to this theory. His model explained human action as the result of four systems:

1. the "behavioral system" of biological needs;
2. the "personality system" of an individual's characteristics affecting their functioning in the social world;
3. the "social system" of patterns of units of social interaction, especially social status and role; and

4. the "cultural system" of norms and values that regulate social action symbolically.

As per this theory, the second system was the proper object of study for psychologists; the third system for sociologists, and the fourth system for cultural anthropologists. Whereas the Boasians considered all of these systems to be objects of study by anthropologists, and "personality" and "status and role" to be as much a part of "culture" as "norms and values," Parsons envisioned a much narrower role for anthropology and a much narrower definition of culture. Although Boasian cultural anthropologists were interested in norms and values, among many other things, it was only with the rise of structural functionalism that people came to identify "culture" with "norms and values." Many American anthropologists rejected this view of culture (and by implication, anthropology).

Notably, combination of American cultural anthropology theory with British social anthropology methods has led to some confusion between the concepts of "society" and "culture." For most anthropologists, these are distinct concepts. Society refers to a group of people; culture refers to a pan-human capacity and the totality of non-genetic human phenomena. Societies are often clearly bounded; cultural traits are often mobile, and cultural boundaries, such as they are, are typically porous, permeable, and plural. During the 1950s and 1960s anthropologists often worked in places where social and cultural boundaries coincided, thus obscuring the distinction. When disjunctures between these boundaries become highly salient, for example during the period of European de-colonization of Africa in the 1960s and 1970s, or during the post-Bretton Woods realignment of globalization, however, the difference often becomes central to anthropological debates.

Remarkably, Clifford Geertz and David M. Schneider, and Roy Wagner, went on to important careers as cultural anthropologists and developed a school within American cultural anthropology called "symbolic anthropology," the study of the social construction and social effects of symbols. Since symbolic anthropology easily complemented social anthropologists' studies of social life and social structure, many British structural-functionalists (who rejected or were uninterested in Boasian cultural anthropology) accepted the Parsonian definition of "culture" and "cultural anthropology." British anthropologist Victor Turner (who eventually left the United Kingdom to teach in the United States) was an important bridge between American and British symbolic anthropology. Attention to symbols, the meaning of which depended almost entirely on their historical and social context, appealed to many Boasians. Leslie White asked of cultural things, "What sort of objects are they? Are they physical objects? Mental objects? Both? Metaphors? Symbols? Reifications?" In *Science of Culture* (1949), he concluded that they are objects "*sui generis*"; that is, of their own kind. In trying to define that kind, he hit upon a previously unrealized aspect of symbolization, which he called "the symbolate"—an object created by the act of symbolization. He thus defined culture as "symbolates understood in an extra-somatic context."

Although White's view echoes that of Malinowski, the key concept for White was not "function" but "adaptation." Whereas the Boasians were interested in the history of specific traits, White was interested in the cultural history of the human species, which he felt should be studied from an evolutionary perspective. Thus, the task of anthropology is to study "not only how culture evolves, but why as well.... In the case of man ... the power to invent and to discover, the ability to select and use the better of two tools or ways of doing something- these are the factors of cultural evolution." Unlike 19th century evolutionists, who were concerned with how civilized societies rose above primitive societies. White was interested in documenting how, over time, humankind as a whole has through cultural means discovered more and more ways for capturing and harnessing energy from the environment, in the process transforming culture. At the same time that White was developing his theory of cultural evolution, Kroeber's student Julian Steward was developing his theory of cultural ecology. In 1938 he published *Basin-Plateau Aboriginal Socio-Political Groups* in which he argued that diverse societies—for example the indigenous Shoshone or White farmers on the Great Plains—were not less or more evolved; rather, they had adapted differently to different environments. Whereas Leslie White was interested in culture understood holistically as a property of the human species, Julian Steward was interested in culture as the property of distinct societies. Like White he viewed culture as a means of adapting to the environment, but he criticized Whites "unilineal" (one direction) theory of cultural evolution and instead proposed a model of "multilineal" evolution in which (in the Boasian tradition) each society has its own cultural history.

It is remarkable that the debate between symbolic and materialist approaches to culture dominated American Anthropologists in the 1960s and 1970s. The Vietnam War and the publication of Dell Hymes' *Reinventing Anthropology*, however, marked a growing dissatisfaction with the then dominant approaches to culture. Hymes argued that fundamental elements of the Boasian project such as holism and an interest in diversity were still worth pursuing: "interest in other peoples and their ways of life, and concern to explain them within a frame of reference that includes ourselves." Moreover, he argued that cultural anthropologists are singularly well-equipped to lead this study (with an indirect rebuke to sociologists like Parsons who sought to subsume anthropology to their own project): In the practice there is a traditional place for openness to phenomena in ways not predefined by theory or design – attentiveness to complex phenomena, to phenomena of interest, perhaps aesthetic, for their own sake, to the sensory as well as intellectual, aspects of the subject. These comparative and practical perspectives, though not unique to formal anthropology, are specially husbanded there, and might well be impaired, if the study of man were to be united under the guidance of others who lose touch with experience in concern for methodology, who forget the ends of social knowledge in elaborating its means, or who are unwittingly or unconcernedly culture-bound..

Boas and Malinowski established ethnographic research as a highly localized method for studying culture. Yet Boas emphasized that culture is dynamic, moving from one group of people to another, and that specific cultural forms have to be analyzed in a larger context. This has led anthropologists to explore different ways of understanding the global dimensions of culture.

In the 1940s and 1950s, several key studies focused on how trade between indigenous peoples and the Europeans who had conquered and colonized the Americas influenced indigenous culture, either through change in the organization of labor, or change in critical technologies. Bernard Mishkin studied the effect of the introduction of horses on Kiowa political organization and warfare. Oscar Lewis explored the influence of the fur trade on Blackfoot culture (relying heavily on historical sources).

Joseph Jablow documented how Cheyenne social organization and subsistence strategy between 1795 and 1840 were determined by their position in trade networks linking Whites and other Indians. Frank Secoy argued that Great Plains Indians' social organization and military tactics changed as horses, introduced by the Spanish in the south, diffused north, and guns, introduced by the British and French in the east, diffused west.

In the 1950s Robert Redfield and students of Julian Steward pioneered "community studies," namely, the study of distinct communities (whether identified by race, ethnicity, or economic class) in Western or "Westernized" societies, especially cities.

They thus encountered the antagonisms 19th century critics described using the terms "high culture" and "low culture." These 20th century anthropologists struggled to describe people who were politically and economically inferior but not, they believed, culturally inferior. Oscar Lewis proposed the concept of a "culture of poverty" to describe the cultural mechanisms through which people adapted to a life of economic poverty. Other anthropologists and sociologists began using the term "sub-culture" to describe culturally distinct communities that were part of larger societies. One important kind of subculture is that formed by an immigrant community. In dealing with immigrant groups and their cultures, there are various approaches:

(a) *Leitkultur (core culture):* A model developed in Germany by Bassam Tibi. The idea is that minorities can have an identity of their own, but they should at least support the core concepts of the culture on which the society is based.

(b) *Melting Pot:* In the USA, the traditional view has

been one of a melting pot where all the immigrant cultures are mixed and amalgamated without state intervention.

(c) *Monoculturalism:* In some European states, culture is very closely linked to nationalism, thus government policy is to assimilate immigrants, although recent increases in migration have led many European states to experiment with forms of multiculturalism.

(d) *Multiculturalism:* A policy that immigrants and others should preserve their cultures with the different cultures interacting peacefully within one nation.

Notably, the way nation-states treat immigrant cultures rarely falls neatly into one or another of the above approaches. The degree of difference with the host culture (i.e., "foreignness"), the number of immigrants, attitudes of the resident population, the type of government policies that are enacted, and the effectiveness of those policies all make it difficult to generalize about the effects. Similarly with other subcultures within a society, attitudes of the mainstream population and communications between various cultural groups play a major role in determining outcomes. The study of cultures within a society is complex and research must take into account a myriad of variables.

In the context of cultural studies, the idea of a *text* not only includes written language, but also films, photographs, fashion or hairstyles: the texts of cultural studies comprise all the meaningful artifacts of culture. Similarly, the discipline widens the concept of "culture". "Culture" for a cultural studies researcher not only includes traditional high culture (the culture of ruling social groups) and popular culture, but also everyday meanings and practices. The last two, in fact, have become the main focus of cultural studies. A further and recent approach is comparative cultural studies, based on the discipline of comparative literature and cultural studies.

Scholars in the United Kingdom and the United States developed somewhat different versions of cultural studies after the field's inception in the late 1970s. The British version of cultural studies was developed in the 1950s and 1960s mainly under the influence first of Richard Hoggart, E. P. Thompson, and Raymond Williams, and later Stuart Hall and others at the Centre for Contemporary Cultural Studies at the University of Birmingham. This included overtly political, left-wing views, and criticisms of popular culture as 'capitalist' mass culture; it absorbed some of the ideas of the Frankfurt School critique of the "culture industry" (i.e. mass culture). This emerges in the writings of early British cultural-studies scholars and their influences: see the work of (for example) Raymond Williams, Stuart Hall, Paul Willis, and Paul Gilroy.

Cultural Change

Obviously, cultural invention has come to mean any innovation that is new and found to be useful to a group of people and expressed in their behavior but which does not exist as a physical object. Humanity is in a global "accelerating culture change period", driven by the expansion of international commerce, the mass media, and above all, the human population explosion, among other factors. Cultures are internally affected by both forces encouraging change and forces resisting change.

These forces are related to both social structures and natural events, and are involved in the perpetuation of cultural ideas and practices within current structures, which themselves are subject to change. Social conflict and the development of technologies can produce changes within a society by altering social dynamics and promoting new cultural models, and spurring or enabling generative action. These social shifts may accompany ideological shifts and other types of cultural change. For example, the U.S. feminist movement involved new practices that produced a shift in gender relations, altering both gender and economic structures. Environmental conditions may also enter as factors. Changes include following for the film local hero.

For example, after tropical forests returned at the end of the last ice age, plants suitable for domestication were available, leading to the invention of agriculture, which in turn brought about many cultural innovations and shifts in social dynamics. Cultures are externally affected via contact between societies, which may also produce—or inhibit—social shifts and changes in cultural practices. War or competition over resources may impact technological development or social dynamics. Additionally, cultural ideas may transfer from one society to another, through diffusion or acculturation. In diffusion, the form of something (though not necessarily its meaning) moves from one culture to another. For example, hamburgers, mundane in the United States, seemed exotic when introduced into China. "Stimulus diffusion" (the sharing of ideas) refers to an element of one culture leading to an invention or propagation in another.

"Direct Borrowing" on the other hand tends to refer to technological or tangible diffusion from one culture to another. Diffusion of innovations theory presents a research-based model of why and when individuals and cultures adopt new ideas, practices, and products.

Acculturation has different meanings, but in this context refers to replacement of the traits of one culture with those of another, such has happened to certain Native American tribes and to many indigenous peoples across the globe during the process of colonization. Related processes on an individual level include assimilation (adoption of a different culture by an individual) and transculturation.

In the preceding discussion, we have made an attempt to portray culture and related issues from an academic and analytic angle. All salient features of culture are amply described.

Now we come to our main theme of the work, human rights in cultural and religious perspective.

What Are Human Rights?

It is pertient to note that the language of Human Rights is comparatively new. It began to take shape in the 18th century. The French Revolution, for instance, issued a Declaration on the Rights of Man in 1789. Prior to that came the Philadelphia Declaration of the Right to Self-determination in 1776. The phrase gained currency in the 19th century, and came to a culmination in the mid 20th century in the U.N. Declaration on Human Rights (1948). Observers have made the point that the 1948 Declaration was a defence of the "West" against Eastern Europe and that the Declaration of 1789 was valid only for Western Europe and not for its colonies which were not yet deemed ready for human rights.

In the like ways, the Right to Self-determination excluded from its purview native Americans and Blacks just as the 1776 Declaration of Independence did. The self-evident truth that all men are created equal did not apply to Native Americans and Blacks. When Washington signed that document, he had in his Vernon estate some 300 slaves and none of whom was set free in the days and years that followed.

It is remarkable that the language of human rights was a product of the European Enlightenment. It was a secular language for a concept of secular origin. But "secular" could have more than one level of meaning. It could denote rejection of control by religious power; independence and freedom from religious ideas and norms; or opposition to religion in any form. One would support the secular rejection of totalitarian control by religious power of human life and activities. Many areas of life have a legitimate autonomy which must be respected. One wonders if anything genuinely human could be wholly independent of, unrelated to, and unconcerned with the religious, that is, the horizons of ultimate meaning.

Completely ignoring religion may lead to an all-round impoverishment of the human, and may deeply hurt the cause of human rights. An analogy might be the bleakness and shallowness that could result from an exclusion or neglect of poetry. Thomas Hobbes banned metaphors; Descartes found poetry irreconcilable with his scientific method; and Plato, surprisingly, would have no poets in his Republic. Poets and artists represent new possibilities for life, beyond the given and the settled, and beyond the law and order of ruling oligarchs. The mere fact of something being secular need not be a scoring point: oppression is also secular as is slavery, colonial plunder and exploitation of the weak. These are anti-religious too. Human rights are secular, in the sense that they are autonomous and earthbound, historically evolving and related to the here and the now. But religion is also secular in the same sense: it has its autonomy, and is for living on this earth within this ongoing history in dialogue with the concrete here and now of life.

Now that means two things, namely the secular and the religious need not be thought of nor lived as mutually exclusive; and human rights should be seen as related both to the secular and to the religious. The history of all religions tell of serious violations of human rights. That should not put us off nor lead us to brush religion aside. A gap between the ideal and the practical, between creed and life is neither uncommon or unknown. It is necessary therefore to explore the core message of each religious tradition, and search for aspects or factors which can and do, support, favour, nourish, even demand and engender human rights. That will be a more profound approach to the issue of human rights and religion. Human rights must be considered in the concrete, in their actual context.

They are not liable to abstract, formal definitions. What points to this is the fact that human rights speech has developed from an expanding social consciousness of their violation. We shall then realize the extreme complexity and variety of human rights, and the ramifications of each into all or most levels of human existence and areas of human concern. The universality and global character of human rights have serious consequences. Reality is interconnected. Life is a web. Life has become much more interlaced today politically, culturally and economically than ever before. What happens in one corner of the earth may not only be known quickly or seen simultaneously everywhere else, but can affect the lives of millions of people in remote villages of another continent. Hence the need of a global ethic and a universal human rights Covenant.

That means we need an agreed basis for human rights, a point of common reference, a symbol which can appeal to every mind and heart. We need one which is not of our making but has independent existence and authority. One which "creates" us and is not created by us. It may be something like Truth which when encountered has claims on us and to which we owe not submission but glad obedience. That reference point or horizon of meaning is what we call God, the Pi vine. Such is the source and guarantee of human rights.

Human rights flowing from such a source have 4 basic contents or concerns: Life, Freedom, Conscience and Relationship These can be further defined as the right to life and the means of living in a manner worthy of human beings. Freedom which is at the heart of life and which defines us as human. It includes a variety of well-known freedoms, among them the freedom to call things, ideas and institutions into question, the freedom to experiment and innovate in favour of a fuller life and dignity, and the freedom to share ideas, compare notes and create a milieu favourable to the sifting and growth of Truth.

The community rather than individuals is the ultimate subject of truth and of human rights. But freedom is to be understood not so much in terms of the possibility of choosing between alternatives as in terms of the capacity to love, to transcend self and live for others, even to the extent of risk-taking and dying that others may live and have life in its fullness. Love is the actualization of freedom.

Remember! Freedom grows, deepens and matures in direct proportion to the growth and maturation of love. And it is love that humanizes us. It realizes itself as justice, compassion/ Karuna, mercy, forgiveness, reconciliation, reverence and celebration of the other. Conscience refers to that deep sense, native to all human persons, of right and wrong, of what may and may not be done said or thought; it is a sense of what gives life and enhances freedom as against what enslaves or kills. Relationship points to the fact that human life is always lived in community. Life is life with others. It is life from and for and with one another. That means human rights are relational and have to do with the existence and interaction of persons in communities and of communities of persons. An individualistic presentation, then, of human rights is unacceptable.

The 1948 document is the West's self-defense against the East and its governing ethos is capitalist individualism which fragments and destroys national and world community, thereby introducing alienation of all from all and from the Earth. Human rights can exist and flourish only within the web of relationships of mutual respect, acceptance, concern and sharing. That means that corresponding to human rights there are human responsibilities. Rights and Responsibilities function like the warp and woof of the social fabric. One may recall that in precapitalist days, in tribal societies and even in Europe's middle ages, rights and responsibilities always went together.

In fact, some modern national constitutions are based on the trinity of liberty, equality and fraternity. In capitalist individualist traditions liberty gets emphasized at the expense of the others; in socialist experiments equality is accepted while liberty and fraternity are sacrificed. In framing the Indian Constitution, Dr. B.R. Ambedkar sought (and he was the first) to hold the three together in dynamic unity, in a perichoresis. But now with India's massive surrender to the free market, equality and fraternity have once again fallen victim to the liberty of the wealthy. Profound human rights violations are involved in this process. All these factors constituting human rights point to and lead to and express what they ultimately derive from, namely, Human Dignity.

Traditional culture is not a substitute for human rights; it is a cultural context in which human rights must be established, integrated, promoted and protected. Human rights must be approached in a way that is meaningful and relevant in diverse cultural contexts. Rather than limit human rights to suit a given culture, why not draw on traditional cultural values to reinforce the application and relevance of universal human rights? There is an increased need to emphasize the common, core values shared by all cultures: the value of life, social order and protection from arbitrary rule. These basic values are embodied in human rights.

In fact, traditional cultures should be approached and recognized as partners to promote greater respect for and observance of human rights. Drawing on compatible practices and common values from traditional cultures would enhance and advance human rights promotion and protection. This approach not only encourages greater tolerance, mutual respect and understanding, but also fosters more effective international cooperation for human rights.

Greater understanding of the ways in which traditional cultures protect the well-being of their people would illuminate the common foundation of human dignity on which human rights promotion and protection stand. This insight would enable human rights advocacy to assert the cultural relevance, as well as the legal obligation, of universal human rights in 'diverse cultural contexts.

Recognition and appreciation of particular cultural contexts would serve to facilitate, rather than reduce, human rights respect and observance. Working in this way with particular cultures inherently recognizes cultural integrity and diversity, without compromising or diluting the unquestionably universal standard of human rights. Such an approach is essential to ensure that the future will be guided above all by human rights, non-discrimination, tolerance and cultural pluralism.

Global Pluralism and Diversity

In fact, Human rights are what make us human. They are the principles by which we create the sacred home for human dignity.

Article 1 of the Universal Declaration of Human Rights (UDHR) states that:

> "All human beings are born free and equal in dignity and rights. They are endowed with reason and conscience and shall act towards one another in a spirit of brotherhood."

Human rights are what reason requires and conscience commands. They are us and we are them. Human rights are rights that any person has as a human being. We are all human beings-, we are all deserving of human rights. One cannot be true without the other.

The absence of tolerance and human rights is not only a denial of human dignity. It is also the root of the suffering and hatred that breeds political violence and inhibits economic development. If this century's history has taught us one lesson, it is this. When we speak of the right to life, or development, or to dissent and diversity, we are speaking of tolerance. Tolerance promoted, protected and enshrined will ensure all freedoms. Without it, we can be certain of none. In the words of one wise man: "Faith elicits respect, and fanaticism provokes hate."

Human rights are the expression of those traditions of tolerance in all cultures that are the basis of peace and progress. Human rights, properly understood and justly interpreted, are foreign to no culture and native to all nations. It is the universality of human rights that gives them their strength and endows them with the power to cross any border, climb any wall, defy force. There is no universal morality, because the history of the world is the story of the plurality of cultures, and the attempt to assert universality, or even the procedural principle of 'universalizability', as a criterion of all morality, is a more or less well-disguised version of the imperial routine of trying to make the values of a particular culture.

In this regard, such documents as the Universal Declaration of Human Rights, passed by the United Nations in 1948, are futile proclamations, derived from the moral principles valid in one culture and thrown out into the moral void between cultures. They might have some validity if the proclaiming culture was successfully imperialist, and had imposed its values on others by force majeure, but the doctrine of cultural relativism at its strongest regards this always as a superficial phenomenon, incapable of eroding the irreducible core of cultural singularity in the various social components of the world. The protest it utters against imperialism, and the buttress it seems to provide against it, are two of the attractions of the doctrine of cultural relativism. It suggests, with Rousseau, that missionaries are no better than conquerors.

Moreover, it seems to carry the fight further, beyond

the country which seeks to impose its culture abroad, to any attitude which suggests the assumption of the moral superiority of self. It questions any view of morality that ascribes an exclusive and exalted position to the morality of one's own society. It is against what is now called ethnocentrism, and it sees in moral self-centredness the formula for a constant battle among cultures, each insisting on its moral superiority. To this it opposes a tolerance based partly on scepticism about the claim of any one culture to wholesale moral superiority, and partly on the claim that the 'recognition of cultural relativity carries with it its own values': namely, the acceptance of the equally valid patterns of life which mankind has created for itself from the raw materials of existence.

Cultural egalitarianism seems to follow from cultural relativism. So the argument provided by cultural relativism against imperialism appeals not merely because it is an argument against imperialism, but because it seems true. There is a plurality of cultures in the world, and these cultures produce their own values.

There are no universal values. This, to the cultural relativist, is not a problem. It is a solution. How does one cope with the coexistence in the world of value-systems that conflict with each other, or which are not necessarily mutually consistent? One adopts Hume's formula: "In each city, the rites of that city."

A second way of drawing the particular and the general together might be to investigate the extent to which the rights of various peoples do in fact overlap, so that there is, as a matter of observation, a core of basic rights that is common to all cultures. And a third way might be to examine the extent to which there exists, in contemporary world society, a single cosmopolitan culture stretched over the profusion of indigenous cultures, so that there is a properly universal level at which the vocabulary of human rights has meaning.

In the next chapter, we will give an elaborate account of multiculturalism and other relevant issues and their impact on human rights.

REFERENCES

Ankerl, Guy (2000). *Global communication without universal civilization, vol.1: Coexisting contemporary civilizations: Arabo-Muslim, Bharati, Chinese, and Western*. INU societal research. Geneva: INU Press.

Arnold, Matthew. (1869). *Culture and Anarchy*. New York: Macmillan. Third edition, 1882, available online. Retrieved: 2006-06-28.

Bakhtin, M.M. (1981) *The Dialogic Imagination: Four Essays*. Ed. Michael Holquist. Trans. Caryl Press.

Barzilai, Gad. (2003). *Communities and Law: Politics and Cultures of Legal Identities* University of Michigan Press.

Bourdieu, Pierre. (1977). *Outline of a Theory of Practice*. Cambridge University Press.

Cohen, Anthony P. (1985). *The Symbolic Construction of Community*. Routledge: New York,

Dawkiins, R. (1982). *The Extended Phenotype: The Long Reach of the Gene*. Paperback ed., 1999. Oxford Paperbacks.

Findley & Rothney (1986). *Twentieth-Century World* Houghton Mifflin.

Forsberg, A. *Definitions of culture* CCSF Cultural Geography course notes. Retrieved: 2006-06-29.

Geertz, Clifford. (1973). *The Interpretation of Cultures: Selected Essays*. New York.

Goodall, J. (1986). *The Chimpanzees of Gombe: Patterns of Behavior*. Cambridge, MA: Belknap Press of Harvard University Press.

Hoult, T.F., ed. (1969). *Dictionary of Modern Sociology*. Totowa, New Jersey, United States: Littlefield, Adams & Co.

Jary, D. and J. Jary. (1991). *The HarperCollins Dictionary of Sociology*. New York: HarperCollins.

2

Multiculturalism and Relevent Issues

> "The superior man thinks always of virtue; the common man thinks of comfort."
>
> —*Confucius*

After having a detailed overview of culture and human rights in the preceding chapter, now we come to multiculturalism and other relevant issues in the context of studying human rights.

Basically, the term 'multiculturalism' covers a number of current political trends in North America and elsewhere which, although they are quite different in their aims and ideological content, share a positive evaluation of cultural traditions and, particularly, the cultural or ethnic identities of minorities. Multiculturalism is evident in literature and the arts as well as in politics, and it seeks to revalorise the artistic and intellectual contributions of hitherto silent minorities as well as supporting their quest for equity in greater society.

Related to the critical Hegelianism of the early Frankfurt School, to feminist critiques of epistemology and to postmodernist trends inspired directly or indirectly by Derrida, multi-culturalist thought is often accused of inspiring nihilism since it seems to relativise absolute value judgements.

Cultural Variation as a Political Challenge

It is pertinent to note that for many years, it was commonplace within post-evolutionist comparative cultural research - cultural and social anthropology to assume that cultures were generally sharply delineated and distinct, relatively homogeneous and stable. The world was thus depicted as a vast archipelago of cultures, each possessing its own internal logic and its own values, and which could exclusively be understood in its own unique terms. Variations in morality, custom and tradition were thus regarded as evidence of people's ability to adapt to the most variable environments and to shape their existence in a multitude of ways, and it was emphasised that there was no 'objective' standard available for the evolutionary ranking of cultures or the moral valuation of actions. Value was defined from within. This fine of thought which is historically associated with the great German-American anthropologist Franz Boas, is usually spoken of as cultural relativism or historical particularism.

Of late, the classic perspectives from cultural relativism have become increasingly problematic (cf. also Wilson's Introduction to this volume), and cultural theory from the 1980s and 1990s tends to emphasise (now approaching the point of irritating reiteration) that, cultures are neither clearly bounded, tightly integrated nor unchanging. An important contributing cause, or at least a major catalyst, in bringing this change about, is the intensification of the globalisation of culture since the World War II.

The recent globalisation of capitalism and the modern state, along with innovations in communication technology (jet planes, cable, TV satellites and various wireless telecommunications are key innovations), have been crucial for these changes to come about. When former 'tribals' now apply for mortgages, follow North American TV series, take their Higher School Certificates, elect local governments and are imprisoned for criticising the government, it becomes intellectually and morally indefensible to seek refuge in the fiction of assuming that cultures are isolated and committed to their 'proper logic': political discourse has, to a great extent, become globalised.

The situation may be even more problematic to handle intellectually for persons steeped in Boasian relativism when very tangible expressions of global cultural variation suddenly appear at our doorstep, which indeed is happening in most industrialised societies due to labour migration and to the ongoing influx of political refugees. This new polyethnic situation has, especially in European countries, provoked discrimination as well as a revitalised cultural nationalism and chauvinism in segments of the majority, but many -'indigenes' as well as new arrivals have also responded by developing ideological and practical models for polyethnic coexistence. Original alloys mixing anthropological cultural relativism, nationalism, modern individualism and human rights thought have thus, in the course of the past 20 years, created ideologies and theories dealing with 'multicultural society'.

In this milieu of social and political thought, difference is seen not only as politically legitimate, but is also frequently invoked as justification for specific political rights. In this regard, multiculturalist thought could be seen as post-nationalist, since it acknowledges the existence of several 'cultures' within one and the same political system. At the same time, multiculturalism may easily conflict with values seen as universal in modern liberal states, especially those to do with human rights and the rights and duties associated with equal participation in the institutions of society. The basic dilemma of polyethnic societies can be phrased like this: on the one hand all members of a liberal democracy are (in principle if not in practice) entitled to the same rights and opportunities.

On the other hand, they also have the right to be different - and in the 1990s, the rights of minorities to maintain and promote their cultural specificity, and to be visible in the public sphere, including the media, school curricula and so on, are increasingly insisted on. A crucial challenge for multi-ethnic societies therefore consists in allowing cultural differences without violating common, societally defined rights; in other words, the challenge consists in finding a viable compromise, for the state as well as for the citizens (representing power and agency, respectively, in the framework proposed in Wilson's Introduction), between equal rights and the right to be different. This contradiction is as old as nationalism itself. Nationalism, the ideology holding that states ought to be culturally homogeneous (Anderson 1983; Gellner 1983), has a double origin in German Romanticism and French Enlightenment thought, which emphasise, respectively, cultural (in many cases ethnic as well) uniformity, and shared territory and citizenship, as the basis for national integration and as the source of political legitimation. According to classic Enlightenment thought, there existed a universal human civilisation, which was in principle accessible to all humans.

As per German Romanticism, represented in the works of Herder above all, every people (Volk) had its proper linguistic and cultural character and the right to defend it.

This view of culture, incidentally, was developed largely as a defensive response to French universalism, which was locally perceived as a form of cultural imperialism (probably not without a certain justification). This perspective and its derivatives (including cultural relativism in its 'strong' variants) are currently expressed through ideologies arguing the importance of cultural homogeneity for political identity. This applies whether they are nationalist and champion the idea of homogeneous states, or ethnopolitical and insist on ethnically based rights for minorities within existing states.

However, the difference between 'German' and 'French' nationalism, so often stressed in the literature (see Kohn 1945 for a classic statement), is not absolute: in actually existing nations, the two principles are generally mixed, and even in principle, French territorialism is far from being culturally innocent. Insofar as the French universalist civilisation insists on speaking French, it has certainly not been perceived as culturally neutral among non-French speakers in Brittany, in Cote d'lvoire and elsewhere, modern human rights thinking is no more neutral either, incidentally, as it assumes global sharing of a specified set of societal values. The contradiction between the demands for equal rights and for the right to be different is accentuated at present by two main tendencies. First, it has finally become dear in public discourse - nearly 80 years after Woodrow Wilson famously announced the right to self-determination of peoples - that hardly any ethnic group has its territory by itself. States are polyethnic, and any ideology stating that only people 'of the same kind' should live in a country is potentially dangerous.

This problem was recognised already by Renan (1992 (1882]), but it has acquired unprecedented importance since the 1960s. Second, the current processes of cultural globalisation break down cultural boundaries and make it difficult to defend the idea that a 'people' is culturally homogeneous and unique. Cultural creolisation (or 'hybridisation', or again 'bastardisation' if one prefers), migration and increased transnational communication are important keywords here.

A widespread counter-reaction against the perceived threat of boundary dissolution through globalisation consists in ideological emphases on 'cultural uniqueness'. In this sense, cultural homogenisation and ethnic fragmentation take place simultaneously; they are consequences of each other and feed on each other in dynamic interplay. In other words, modern societies are by default 'multicultural'- or so it may seem.

It shall nevertheless be argued that 'multiculturalist polities' have to be universalistic in their very nature. The position to be defended below argues that culture is not a legitimating basis for political claims, and that cultural singularities among minorities and majorities in modern societies can only be defended to the extent that they do not interfere with individual human rights. All societies are indeed 'multicultural', whether they contain diverse ethnic groups or not, since different citizens hold different values and different world views. Multiculturalism, a term describing doctrines which argue the importance and equivalence of cultural heritages and the decentralisation of defining power as to what is to count as one, may in practice be a strong form of individualistic thinking about personhood - the world seen as a smorgasbord of identity options. This kind of thinking, described as 'critical multiculturalism'by Turner (1994), may enable diverse groups to participate in public life, with their 'cultural heritage' or 'cultural identity' as their legitimated symbolic capital, and it can thereby be liberating for formerly silenced or unarticulate groups, including non-ethnic groups such as women and homosexuals. If, on the other hand, institutionalised differences form the core of multiculturalist practices, it is liable to regress into nihilism, apartheid and/ or the enforced ascription of cultural identities.

Culture, Raymond Williams has written (1976) in a much quoted passage, is one of the two or three most complex words of the English language. The meaning of the word, Williams shows, has gone through many changes since the original Latin colere, which referred to the cultivation of the soil. Today, the word has several, if related, meanings. One of the most common meanings of culture posits it as synonymous with the way of life and world view the members of a particular group or community have in common, and which distinguishes them from other groups. This definition may at first seem plausible, but it does not survive closer scrutiny. Within nearly every 'group' or 'people' there are varying ways of life and world views; the rich differ from the poor, the men from the women, the highly educated from the illiterate, the urban from the rural and so on. Additionally, it is often extremely difficult to draw boundaries between 'cultures'.

If one argues that a Norwegian culture exists and is by default different from Danish culture, one will need to show what it is that all Norwegians share with each other but not with a single Dane. That is not an easy thing to do. Finally, culture is naturally not a solid object, even if the word unhappily is a noun. Culture is something which happens, not something that merely exists; it unfolds through social process and therefore also inherently changes. Problems of this kind have made such a conceptualisation of culture difficult to manage, and many scholars have ceased to use it, while others insist on using culture in the singular sense, seen as that which all humans have in common, defining them as a species as opposed to nature in general and other species in particular.

However, ideologists and political entrepreneurs of many shades have embraced this Romantic concept of culture. In recent years, ‚culture' and 'cultural identity' have become important tools for the achievement of political legitimacy and influence in many otherwise very different societies - from Bolivia to Siberia. It is used by political leaders of hegemonic majorities as well as by the spokesmen of weak minorities. Indigenous peoples all over the world demand territorial rights from the states in which they live, emphasising their unique cultural heritage and way of life as a crucial element in their plea.

Immigrant leaders in Europe occasionally present themselves as the representatives of cultural minorities, demanding, inter alia, special linguistic and religious rights. The hegemonic elites of many countries also refer to their 'national culture' in justification of warfare or oppression of ethnic minorities. 'Cultural pleas' are, in other words, put to very different political uses. A frequently mentioned 'paradox' concerning the break-up of Yugoslavia and subsequent war is the fact that the fighting parties, Serbs, Croats and Bosnian Muslims, are culturally very similar, yet justify their mutual hatred by claiming that they are actually profoundly different.

This kind of situation, where ethnic relations between groups which are culturally close take on a bitter and antagonistic character, is more common than is widely assumed. In Trinidad, in the southern Caribbean, the following development has taken place in recent years (Eriksen 1992). The two largest ethnic groups, Africans and Indians (originally from India; they are not American Indians), have gradually acquired more and more in common, culturally speaking; in terms of language, way of life, ambitions and general outlook.

At the same time, they have become ever more concerned to express how utterly different they are; culture and cultural differences are spoken about more often, and cultural differences are brought to bear on daily life, public rituals and political organisation to a greater extent than was earlier the case. Partly, this is because the groups are in closer contact than earlier and compete for the same scarce resources; but it is also partly because members of the two groups feel that their cultural boundaries are threatened by tendencies towards creolisation and therefore feel an acute need to advertise their cultural differences. The groups have simultaneously become more similar and more different. This paradox is characteristic of globalisation processes, whereby differences between peoples are made comparable and therefore come to resemble each other, and where 'small' differences are 'enlarged'. It could, in line with this, be said that the entire discourse over 'multiculturalism' is embedded in a shared cultural framework encompassing, and bringing out the contradictions between, the Romantic notion of culture and the Enlightenment notion of individual rights.

To put it somewhat more crudely, to make demands on behalf of a self-professed 'culture' indicates that one subscribes to a shared global political culture. The logic of multiculturalism and ethnopolitics shares its dual origins with the logic of nationalism in the Enlightenment and Romantic thought of early modem Europe.

Liberalism, Rights and Identity

The 1948 UN Universal Declaration contained a number of articles relating to 'socio-economic' and 'cultural' rights. In 1948, however, the definition of cultural rights focused on education and the right to participate in 'cultural life' in the sense of the arts and sciences, rather than on respecting cultural difference and making redress to colonised peoples. The modernist ethnocentrism of the Universal Declaration rested, as so many commentators have noted, on foundations in Western conceptions of society and 'natural law'. Its authors unreflectively assumed that rights should be vested in individuals rather than collectivities (Messer 1993), and some of the articles, such as Sixteen, which deals with marriage and the family, showed scant concern for non-Western sensibilities. The articles on socio-economic rights were an expression of liberal as well as socialist voices within the Western tradition which argued that 'market society' could not be left to secure human welfare unassisted.

Although they were essentially a charter for welfare state and labour policies which became a matter of broad consensus within the post-war metropolitan capitalist world, they seemed radical enough at the time for the United States to refuse to ratify the legal instruments for their implementation. Today this consensus seems increasingly formal rather than real in the wake of the neo-liberal offensive which accompanied the abandonment of the Fordist-Keynesian mode of economic regulation in the old core industrial economies.

In the aftermath of the collapse of communism and widespread disenchantment of metropolitan 'progressives' with Marxist grand narratives of historical progress and emancipation, many on the left have come to see 'welfarism' in a more positive light, seeing struggles to defend welfare rights not simply as a means of pursuing 'class struggle' within a capitalist order which has been immeasurably strengthened by the collapse or market transformation of the 'actually existing' socialisms, but as positively empowering bases for building new multi-class mass movements and advancing the interests of women.

The view of the capitalist state implicit in this position is more positive (and instrumentalist) than that enshrined in the writings of Marx, It is also broadly consistent with a trend towards replacing the old politics of class with a new politics of 'rights' based on a politics of identity.

As Richard Wilson points out in his introduction to this volume, some examples of rights-based movements, such as the indigenous movement in Guatemala, do not focus their campaigns on national state institutions but on transnational institutions and agencies, since they represent groups which have been historically excluded from participation in national politics. Yet the global role of the United Nations agencies and non-governmental organisations poses the same questions of how 'power inhabits meaning' as the role of the national state. The Northern progressives who see struggles to defend welfare rights as intrinsically emancipating have, as Wendy Brown puts it largely foresaken analyses of the liberal state and capitalism as sites of domination and have focused instead on their implication in social and economic inequalities. At the same time, progressives have implicitly assumed the relatively unproblematic instrumental value of the state and capitalism in addressing inequalities.

Liberalism, Individualism and Social Justice

It is pertinent to note that Liberalism is a far from

Uniform doctrine as far as conceptions of social justice are concerned. Some 'libertarian' neo-liberal theorists whose names are frequently invoked by the New Right, notably Friedrich Hayek, have regarded any redistributive principle of justice as incompatible with liberty and deny meaning to the very term social justice itself in 'a society of free men whose members are allowed to use their own knowledge for their own purposes'. Hayek's definition of 'freedom' as 'the state in which a man is not subject to coercion by the arbitrary will of another or others' (in Lukes 1991), can lead to conclusions of the following kind on the issue of 'basic socio-economic rights':

> "Person who cannot afford to buy food may well have a justifiable grievance which ought to be rectified politically, but it would be misleading [sic] to describe his grievance as lack of freedom".

The point, as far as libertarians are concerned, is that freedom means personal autonomy or full 'self-ownership', a concept which was integral to the Enlightenment view of freedom'; the hungry man is not deprived of his own freedom where his poverty is the unintended consequence of others acting within their rights. Hayek, indeed, would be likely to reject even the idea that the hungry man's situation should be rectified politically, since the implementation of any scheme of distribution based on a concept of 'social justice' is, in his view, dependent on a central authority's coercive imposition of its own assessment of the needs of different individuals or group, and thereby leads down the path to totalitarianism. The libertarian takes inequality of resource endowments between individuals as a normal (natural) condition.

The hungry man could only claim that his 'rights' had

been violated and that his hunger was a consequence of lack of freedom if someone had coercively and arbitrarily imposed his condition - by stealing his wallet, for example. In this rigorously methodological individualist conception, involuntary, structurally imposed situations are convenient fictions dreamed up by totalitarian wolves masquerading as liberal humanist sheep.

In fact, these extraordinarily narrow conceptual restrictions seem designed to close off all possibilities of debating the kinds of questions raised by egalitarians:

> "Are lives not also rendered less autonomous by unintended actions, by social relationships and by impersonal and anonymous processes that may radically restrict people's alternatives of thought and action, and may even shape people's beliefs and preferences: and also by the lack of resources, including skills and motivations? Why ... should we conceive of their 'essential interests' as what narrowly conceived rights protect and narrowly conceived opportunities promote?
>
> Why should they not include basic needs, or the conditions of normal 'functioning', and their access to wider opportunities and a fuller life, and why should these not have a more claim society's resources to the extent to which they remain unmet?
>
> And why, finally, should the domain of disadvantage that is beyond their control - comprising luck, on the one hand, and exploitation on the other - be thought of as the 'natural' background to the practice of non-discrimination, or equal consideration, rather than as the field in which it should be practised?

Yet the libertarians' conceptualisations bear a recognisable relationship to the seven assumptions of 'Possessive Individualism' defined by C.B. Macpherson in his classic study of seventeenth-century thought, the central premise of which is that 'society consists of a series of market relations'.

Their extremity results from insisting that only facts about individuals are acceptable as foundations for explanations of social processes (since 'society does not exist') and the axiomatic nature of their specific view of property rights: that individuals have an unrestricted right to an unlimited quantity of any goods they may accumulate by exercising their personal capacities, In many ways, this is a return to the ideas of the dawn of the capitalist era. It was Locke who contributed the defence of the moral rationality of unlimited accumulation to an emergent liberal doctrine. Locke's position is all the more remarkable because his argument begins by appearing to set limits on individual appropriation on the grounds that: 'Men, being once born, have a right to their Preservation, and consequently to Meat and Drink, and such other things, as Nature affords for their Subsistence' (Second Treatise of Government, cited in Macpherson 1962).

If everyone has the right to preservation in this sense, then it appears that no one should appropriate more than he or she needs, since this prejudices the preservation of others. This was indeed Locke's position as far as the appropriation of produce and land was concerned in 'the First Ages of the World'. Locke proceeds to argue, however, that these rules of 'natural law' ceased to apply, when, still in the state of nature, human beings voluntarily introduced money. Money, unlike perishable natural products, is an asset which never spoils. It is therefore rational to accumulate it (along with land) as capital, overcoming one of the grounds for denying individuals surpluses above their immediate needs (Macpherson 1962).

But the other apparent natural law barrier to unlimited individual accumulation, the argument that accumulating land may deprive others of the right to preservation, appears more intractable. Locke overcame this difficulty by arguing that larger and 'improved' extensions of land increased the 'common stock' of mankind through their superior productivity. He then assumes that the enlarged (individually appropriated) product will be distributed in such a way as to ensure that people left without sufficient land to maintain themselves will be guaranteed at least a basic livelihood as labourers and suggests that, they will in fact enjoy a higher standard of living as a result of increased (social) productivity. Since the rights of all to enough land for subsistence were derived from a more fundamental right to self-preservation and subsistence, Locke can argue that class-divided societies are perfectly consistent with natural law. By introducing the institutional infrastructure of both merchant and agrarian capitalism into his 'state of nature' (Macpherson 1962).

Locke not only provides an apparent moral basis for capitalism, but projects back into a state of nature a difference of rationality between classes which he used to justify the political exclusion of the labouring class and its subjection to both legal sanctions and a tutelary Church. This is the consummate naturalisation of differences in social power within civil society. The difference in the moral and reasoning capacities of the propertied and labouring classes derives from their distinct conditions of life: wage-workers cannot develop their capacities for reason and moral life because they are preoccupied by the exigencies of a hand-to-mouth existence.

If, however, 'by nature', all men are equally capable of shifting for themselves, those who fail behind only have themselves to blame. Thus it became 'possible to reconcile' the justice of the market with the traditional notions of commutative and distributive justice' (Macpherson 1962). A number of the sleights of hand in Locke's argument continue to underpin contemporary argument in bourgeois societies. An obvious one is the assumption that gains in social productivity achieved through private accumulation will be distributed throughout society in such a way as to benefit all those who are disadvantaged. Admittedly, Locke's judgements on these matters oscillated between the realistic and the patently ideological: English labourers are living like the Kings of primitive lands on one page and too close to the subsistence to entertain a rational thought or resist depravity on another.

Yet be did at least recognise that distribution was an issue which needed addressing, and continued to maintain a theory of natural rights to basic subsistence, in contrast to libertarians who try to put the issue beyond debate. The fantasies of 'natural rights' theorists did not, however, prove acceptable to a later generation of liberal theorists taking their lead from Bentham, whose 'principle of utility' was developed in direct opposition to the Declaration of Rights produced by the French Revolution, In the hands of John Stuart Mill, utilitarianism focused on 'social utility' (Bobbio 1990: 59), and his late writings sought to reconcile liberalism and socialism. Mill was, however, wedded, like all liberals, to the idea that state intervention represents a potential menace to the self-realising and self-creating capacities of individuals. His version of utilitarian doctrine asserts that the state may only legitimately interfere with the pursuit of an individual's interests and projects if they are harmful to others, and it is anti-paternalist in the sense that actions which cause harm solely to the individual concerned should not be sanctioned.

The boundary between public and private drawn by Mill therefore tends, in principle, towards a relatively libertarian position, yet there is a twist, since, like Locke (and indeed, Aristotle), Mill did not regard 'barbarous' segments of humanity as worthy subjects for such freedoms, because their faculties and capacities were insufficiently developed (Bobbio 1990:61).

Within societies which had achieved a degree of 'progress', universal education could, Mill thought, eventually justify the inclusion of the labouring classes in the franchise, but illiteracy and dependence on parish relief remained valid reasons for excluding persons from participation in government; Mill's notion of liberal democracy even countenanced the idea that the better-educated should be entitled to more than one vote. Furthermore, the 'social' version of utilitarianism could itself be paternalist: Mill argued that women should have the vote because, as the weaker sex, they were more in need of society's protection if they were not to suffer harm at the hands of men (Bobbio 1990: 65).

Nineteenth-century political liberalism therefore by no means equates with democracy, and Mill's emphasis on maximising the happiness of all citizens preserves the fundamentals of earlier individualistic formulations whilst leaving the question of who is to make the decisions about the 'social good' uncomfortably ill-defined. What does, however, emerge from Mill's model of 'historical progress' and 'improvement' is an argument for the (eventual) inclusion of the lower (working and tax-paying) classes in the political community, along with the idea that the political representation of a plurality of conflicting interests is a pre-condition not merely for avoiding 'despotism' but for securing continuing progress. Macpherson argued that the political exclusion of the working classes — in effect, the denial of their individualism - was what spurred attempts to -reformulate the liberal problematic in the centuries after Locke, and made the tensions between liberalism, democracy and social equality increasingly central to the debate.

Yet the problems confronting the modern capitalist metropolis again seem to be one of the relationship between social exclusion and political representation and participation, as growing proportions of the populations resident within national territories occupy social positions which less and less resemble the 'improving' working classes which Mill felt were proper subjects for enfranchisement. At the forefront of modern attempts to reconcile liberal concerns with liberty and social equality is the work of John Rawls, which represents the antithesis of the Hayekian neo-liberal position.

Rawls's theory begins from the premise that the citizens of modern societies are generally divided by differing 'comprehensive doctrines' of the good, that is, that they support deeply conflicting religious, philosophical and moral conceptions. Given these profound differences, Rawls asks how a just and stable society of free and equal citizens can endure. He argues that 'political liberalism' in his terms provides the only viable solution to this dilemma because it provides a basis for social cooperation based around an 'overlapping consensus' which does not entail society uniting around any one comprehensive doctrine.

Rawls concedes, however, that the liberal state cannot avoid taking actions which may have the practical effect of diminishing support for particular comprehensive doctrines and certain forms of life as it strives to sustain social cooperation.

He also recognises that there may be practical difficulty in pre-venting state actions designed to ensure that all citizens understand the substance of their constitutional and civic rights from simultaneously inculcating substantive values of 'autonomy' and self-realising individualism, values which belong to a comprehensive liberal doctrine of the kind advocated by Kant or Mill rather than to the more limited set of virtues and values necessary for an overlapping consensus. An example of the latter type of problem would be the compulsory public education, of children born to parents who were members of religious sects which were radically opposed to the kinds of 'modern' values embodied in the curriculum. Nevertheless, Rawls argues, the aim of political liberalism (as distinct from a comprehensive liberal doctrine) is not to favour one comprehensive doctrine over another, but to secure the conditions for authentic pluralism. This will, however, inevitably lead to the extinction of any conceptions of the good which actually conflict with the principles of justice embodied in political liberalism (such as slavery); furthermore, some forms of life will disappear simply because they will progressively lose adherents because of their incompatibility with the public culture of constitutional democratic regimes.

In accepting that 'social influences favoring some doctrines over others cannot be avoided by any view of political justice', Rawls concedes that- 'We may indeed lament the limited space, as it were, of social worlds, and of ours in particular; and we may regret some of the inevitable effects of our culture and social structure'. He thus at best treats what might, from a different theoretical perspective, be defined as the 'normalising' tendencies of modern disciplinary societies (Brown 1995) as a matter of unavoidable sociological fact, whilst conceding that the liberal state cannot be 'neutral' in significant respects.

Rawls is, however, a strong advocate of redistributive policies, seeking to reconcile liberty and equality with a theory of 'justice as fairness' which rests on methodological individualist premises. Rawls supposes that all members of a democratic society have a rational plan of life which enables them to allocate their personal resources so as to pursue their conceptions of the good over a complete life, taking into account 'reasonable expectations' of their future circumstances. Society itself is seen as a 'fair system of cooperation over time, from one generation to the next'; the conception of political justice defines what terms of cooperation are fair; all persons are 'free' in the sense that they possess powers of moral judgement and reason; and they are 'equal' in the sense that they possess them to the minimum degree necessary to be fully cooperating members of society. In order to free the discussion from 'distracting details', Rawls also treats societies as closed, self-sufficient and temporally self-reproducing systems, which people enter on birth and leave on death, their ability to plan rationally over a complete life being dependent on both this closure and self-sufficiency. He envisages any extension of his theory of justice beyond these constraining assumptions as a matter of addressing just relations between peoples'.

Rawls thus frames the problem of justice in terms of the national state and the rights of its citizens, excluding consideration of the rights of non-citizens and the problems posed by agencies and populations which move across national boundaries. Given that framework however, he argues that only an egalitarian form of liberalism can serve as the basis for a stable system of social cooperation based on overlapping consensus. This entails not merely equal basic rights and liberties and fair rather than' formal equality of opportunity, but also the 'difference principle': 'that the social and economic inequalities attached to offices and positions are to be adjusted so that, whatever the level of those inequalities, they are to the greatest benefit of the least advantaged members of society'. Justice as fairness thus requires an equalisation of life chances and the maximisation of benefits to the least advantaged.

Unless the 'basic needs' of citizens are met, they will be unable to understand and 'fruitfully exercise' their rights and the liberties. Some interpret this as an argument for socialism, although Rawls himself rejects this inference. Working out of what citizens 'need' to fulfil their roles as moral and rational cooperating members of society cannot, however, rest on any comprehensive doctrine of the good (the domain of value conflict within the 'reasonable pluralism' which Rawls regards as integral to democratic society). He therefore draws up a list of 'primary goods' which represent a partial similarity in the structure of citizens' permissible conceptions of the good.

These include freedom of movement and choice of occupation, income and wealth and 'the social bases of self-respect'; they offer a 'practicable public basis of interpersonal comparisons based on objective features of citizens' social circumstances. The purpose of the list is to construct an index against which we can measure the extent to which societies' 'basic structures'- their main political, social and economic institutions - deliver to all citizens the means for 'the adequate development and exercise of their moral powers and a fair share of the all-purpose means essential for advancing their determinate (permissible) conceptions of the good'. Primary goods thus provide a baseline for implementing the Difference Principle.

Rawls's account of primary goods as a condition for the 'normal functioning' of a citizen in a system of social cooperation takes up many of the issues raised earlier in Lukes's list of questions egalitarians would ask of the libertarians. It remains questionable, however, whether it is possible to construct indices of this kind which are flexible enough.

As Lukes observes, variations in the conditions of individuals which limit their real opportunities in life, and are therefore candidates for compensation in the interests of fairness in Rawls's sense, are diverse in their causes and in the forms of compensation which would seem appropriate or reasonable. Is incapacitation by illness or accident, for example, always a matter of individual bad luck rather than socially determined disadvantage, and what form and level of compensation is required? Furthermore, in actually existing constitutional democracies, it seems clear that the level of practical consensus on what claims it is appropriate for citizens to make on 'society' and what 'society' is obliged to deliver is formal rather than real in areas that are central to the notion of 'primary goods'.

First, reductions in welfare compensation to the elderly and unemployed are justified by principles of 'fairness' to taxpayers to which many taxpayers can readily be induced to subscribe, and programmes of 'positive discrimination' tend to provoke backlashes. To some extent these represent a spontaneous clash of values (premised on differentiation of social positions) but they can also be politically orchestrated by a variety of actors ranging from the 'respectable politicians' of the right to racist and fascist organisations beyond the frontiers of institutional party politics.

As argued earlier, even if we restrict ourselves to the political field defined by 'respectable' party politics, we need to recognise that an electorally significant 'consensus' has now been produced in favour of policies which diminish enjoyment of 'basic rights' in countries such as the United States. Whether or not most electors fully subscribe to what this appears to entail -acceptance of the substantive values embedded in neo-liberal comprehensive doctrines - is less important in practice than how they respond to the kinds of 'choices' offered to them by those who are effective players in politics.

In both the United States and Britain, the range of what is on offer from the major political parties has now narrowed to the point where the dominant discourses of mainstream political life share an emphasis on limiting welfare provision to the 'truly needy' and encouraging 'responsibility'. In this kind of framework, redistributive policies go off the agenda, the persistence of poverty and low wages is accepted, and the debate on 'basic rights' becomes a question of entitlement and the division of public and private responsibilities. The state, speaking in the name of 'society', now argues that (normalised) families have private responsibilities towards individuals which should not be transferred to society at large, and that local 'communities' must shoulder more of the burden of care of the poor and incapacitated within their midst.

At the same time, a remorseless insistence on individual responsibility not merely constructs certain categories of welfare subjects (such as unmarried mothers) as morally undeserving, but enjoins us to be good Rawlsians by' making long-term private financial provision for our care in age and infirmity. There are some evident ironies here. The poor have been stereotypically accused of living 'without thought for the future' (and castigated in the past for practices which suggested they did otherwise, such as having large families).

Yet they are clearly not capable of 'planning for the future' by buying that security which the market can offer, and the fact that others are able to protect themselves in this way not merely ameliorates the fiscal problems of the late capitalist state but reinforces the moral stigmatisation of poverty - through discourses of personal responsibility which at the same time ethically validate voting on lines of immediate self-interest.

Second, conflicts over rights which involve appeals to 'fairness' do not necessarily simply involve individuals (singly or as members of a socio-economic category), but may involve more intractable claims based on collective rights and fundamental arguments about the virtues of different forms of life. Rawls assumes that the overlapping consensus common to exponents of different comprehensive conceptions of the good creates a framework in which these differences can be tolerated and rationally discussed, Yet this assumption seems more plausible in his abstract philosopher's world of rational individuals in dosed citizen-societies than in the fractured social worlds which frame postcolonial rights politics, where sustained refusal of real equality and fundamental capitalist interests intervene.

Third, experience of persistent discrimination can erode the foundations for overlapping consensus even between citizens. This is particular clear in the case of the Black population of the United States, much of which is manifesting an increasingly separatist consciousness and rejecting the core symbols of 'national unity. Poverty alone clearly does not explain this situation: Nations, fare worse than Blacks on aggregate in terms of the kind of poverty indicators. It is difficult to know what would have happened in the United States had the policies which created large urban concentrations of poor Blacks not been implemented, but the limited fruits of the politics of Black civil rights and social advancement have now created a climate in which a dialogue in terms of shared commitments to Rawlsian 'political virtues' may no longer be possible. Today; even delivery of more jobs, let alone more welfare, might not be sufficient to assuage accumulated feelings of oppression and exclusion.

Finally, even some of the actions which Rawls proposes to combat disadvantage and apply the Difference Principle require closer scrutiny: the radical forms of social engineering which some deem necessary to eliminate structural causes of the 'lack of capability' to function 'normally' in society attributed to the so-called 'urban underclass' seem problematic because they imply the 'normalcy' of forms of life and behaviour which are part of a hegemonic (and class-based) 'comprehensive conception of the good'.

To what extent are 'features of citizens' social circumstances' truly 'objective', rather than effects of the taxonomic practices of bureaucratic power? If constitutional democracies are not characterised simply by a 'reasonable pluralism' of conceptions of the good but by structures of power which do seek to impose 'comprehensive doctrines' on members of society, then it makes little sense to start with individuals or even groups pursuing conceptions of the good which are seen as their property, competing for support on a level playing field.

Remarkably, Richard Rorty has argued that the merit of Rawls's philosophy is that it is thoroughly historicist and anti-universalist, beginning with liberal democratic society as it exists historically and looking for the ideas and principles actually implicit in its known convictions, such as religious toleration and rejection of slavery. Rawls does not attempt to ground his conception of justice in metaphysics or a view of man's essential nature. Thus 'no such discipline as "philosophical anthropology" is required as a preface to politics, but only history and sociology'. Yet it is a particular kind of history and sociology. Even if one believes that the framework of liberal democracy offers the best prospects history has produced for addressing questions of justice and fairness in social affairs, it remains an open question whether real history is really going the way of Rawls and Rorty on the basis of the evidence have presented thus far on the realities and politics of poverty, even in the countries which come closest to realising liberal ideals.

A major problem raised by Rawls's argument is that of defining 'reasonable pluralism'. Many other liberals who follow Mill in asserting the need for civilised societies to address problems of socio-economic inequality also follow him in emphasising the dangers posed for 'the development of man [sic] as creative and self-directing beings' by any kind of state-directed social project. Isaiah Berlin, for example, writes:

> "Today, the very virtues of even the best-intentioned paternalistic state, its genuine anxiety to reduce destitution -and disease and inequality, to penetrate

> all the neglected nooks and crannies of life which may stand in need of its justice and bounty ... have narrowed the area within which the individual may commit blunders and curtailed his liberties in the interest (the very real interest) of his welfare or his sanity, his health, his security, his freedom from want and fear. His area of choice has grown smaller ... in order to create a situation in which the very possibility of opposed principles, with all their unlimited capacity to cause mental strew and danger and destructive collisions, is eliminated in favour of a simpler and better regulated life, a robust faith in an efficiently working order, untroubled by agonizing moral conflict".

Notably, the Berlin's response to modernity's 'iron cage' is to suggest that:

> What the age calls for is not (as we are so often told) more faith, or stronger leadership, or more scientific organization. Rather it is the opposite - less Messianic ardour, more enlightened scepticism, more toleration of idiosyncrasies, more frequent ad hoc measures to achieve aims in a foreseeable future, more room for the attainment of their personal ends by individuals and by minorities whose tastes and beliefs find (whether rightly or wrongly must not matter) little response among the majority.

Berlin thus insists that minorities (rather than simply individuals) should be allowed more space than that allowed by Rawls: freedom means expanding the space of our social worlds.

In fact, the movement for indigenous rights represents

a stem test of what liberal societies can offer 'minorities'. In at least some cases, indigenous movements challenge a central liberal principle: that rights are ultimately enjoyed by individuals who remain equal under the law but may be assigned special rights as individuals in a certain category. In the current negotiations between the Zapatista Army of National Liberation (EZLN) and the Mexican government in Chiapas, a central demand is to give, communities rather than the individuals which constitute them a legal personality. Abolishing the legal personality of indigenous communities was one of the chief objectives of nineteenth-century liberalism in Mexico and other parts of Latin America.

Although agrarian reform partially undid the privatisation of communal land effected under liberal reforms, the official indigenista ideology of the post-revolutionary Mexican state was assimilationist. 'Material progress'- delivery of basic socio-economic rights - was offered as a compensation for extinction of indigenous identities in favour of a single 'national' identity.

Social Justice in Late Capitalist Societies

It is remarkably that the decline of the welfare state at the expense of abandoning 'critical analyses of state paternalism and state management of capitalism's inequities' is not a viable position because the forms of power embodied in the liberal state produce subjects in Foucault's sense, recodifying boundaries and extending protection to categories of persons defined by and in regulatory discourses. The neo-liberal discourse of the 'minimalist state' might be seen as a mask for expanded state domination, and its accompanying programmes of deregulation, privatisation and 'outsourcing' as new and more effective techniques for managing a social body dismembered by capitalist restructuring. From this standpoint it could be argued that the current interest of the liberal state in giving space to 'indigenous rights' movements and other forms of 'identity polities' fits into a broader picture of the liberal state as a regulatory agency under late capitalist conditions, whose language of recognition of difference as no difference ... becomes a vehicle of subordination through individualization, normalization and regulation, even as it strives to produce visibility and acceptance'. Let us briefly review the problem of 'basic needs'. One of the problems with any theory of 'basic needs' is that it tends to embody minimalist assumptions about what human beings deserve.

Peasant beneficiaries of development projects, for example, have long learned that middle-class bureaucrats think that peasants deserve to subsist, but not to become middle-class themselves. It also seems odd to argue the need to promote 'self-help' among the poor, as if they possessed little intrinsic initiative, given the incredible amount of effort. It has always taken to survive economically in the lower ranks of capitalist society. One of the things history and ethnography seem to teach us about the poor is that they also invest a considerable amount of energy in maintaining their social dignity, not merely in the eyes of their peers, but in their interactions with their superiors (whether the superiors recognise that the exchange has that significance or not). It is therefore not entirely true that one cannot lead a dignified life in conditions of poverty, though it will be certainly be a life which contains many moments of humiliation and physical and emotional suffering. Nevertheless, many of the ways in which people 'contest' their humiliation and individuation, through violent and non-violent means, can be seen as effects of structures of domination and may be as destructive of the person as taking refuge in crack cocaine. Although modern states may be spending more on instruments of social containment in general, the chief targets of repressive legislation and state violence are organised groups, not least the organisations of supposedly moribund 'working classes'. The poor remain relatively powerless, and the politics of social welfare are a powerful legitimation of the state's protectionist role which, in draining poor people of autonomous identities and social diversity, deepens that powerlessness. The 'self-help' alternative to 'paternalism' is also generally individualising, as is the need of many to participate in the 'black' and 'grey' areas of the economy to survive. Both state tactics inhibit politicisation along fundamental fines of class cleavage.

This is why it is far from clear that a politics of rights focused on other kinds of identities - specific forms of injury, discrimination and social subordination on grounds of race, gender or sexual preference, for example - is any more emancipating: seeking redress through the law 'fixes the identities of the injured' as victims of injustice and 'casts the law in particular and the state more generally as neutral arbiters of injury rather than themselves invested with the power to injure'. To challenge domination, that is, to go beyond reactive 'resistance' within the framework of the existing order of domination, requires more than an appeal to the moral sensibilities and reason of the powerful.

It requires a struggle not only for an alternative 'comprehensive conception of the good', but, as Brown puts it, 'an aspiration to power rather than a tendency to reproach it'. Increasing socio-cultural pluralism is not a conspicuous feature of the metropolitan countries of the North at the present time. It is true that some concessions have been made to internally colonised groups within national state borders, but there has been an equally obvious attempt to revalorise a notion of 'national' (majoritarian) culture, accompanied by increasingly strong measures against immigrants, asylum-seekers and refugees who might further 'dilute' national identity.

As Michael Kearney has argued, the formation of transnational migrant populations problematises the regulation of their identities by the bureaucratic and disciplinary apparatuses of national states, but the unequal powers embedded in different national states stiff structure their lives in important ways. It is difficult not to relate these developments to capitalist restructuring. Technological change and shifts in the centres of gravity of the world economy are leaving large segments of the potential 'native' metropolitan work force unemployable in those sectors where higher earnings can still be secured; relocation of production and investment outside national frontiers is undermining the security of skilled working and middle classes accustomed to rising material standards of consumption.

It is not, however, simply shifts within the capitalist world system which make it increasingly hard to envisage a move back to redistributive policies in old or declining 'cores' at the present time. The political base for such policies has been eroded within democratic electoral regimes by the desire of professional politicians to appease 'the middle' as far as possible in the process of transition and to give such a strategy a moral basis. Since the liberal tradition embodies positions which are appropriate for such a purpose, we now find social democrats drawn into a consensus which has shifted towards the right of the possible spectrum of positions.

To the extent that socio-economic marginalisation has 'racial' dimensions (as it clearly does in Britain, Europe and the United States), the short-term advantages of attempts to 'reunite the nation' around a spurious majoritarian construction of 'national culture' is likely to exacerbate conflicts grounded in ethnic communities and the construction of antagonistic 'comprehensive conceptions of the good' of a 'foundationalist' kind. In the last analysis, however, what is happening in the old industrial core zones of the world economy is an intelligible consequence of the need to manage economic decline within the framework of preserving an existing class structure and maintaining the incomes of its upper strata. The non- Western world is bound up with these processes of global economic restructuring in different ways, confronting them through distinct cultures of capitalism, sometimes under the aegis of elites which proclaim their rejection of liberal values.

Given the legacies of history, one might argue that even the Latin American countries where the ethnic divide was deepest, such as Guatemala and Peru, are making strides towards achieving major gams in pluralism relative to the past, in the sense that indigenous peoples are achieving a political voice on the national stage. Mexico's human rights record has certainly not improved under the present administration but one might nevertheless argue that it is a positive development that human rights issues are debated in public and that the dialogue on indigenous rights is taking place.

It is argued, however, that a key issue is how demands for indigenous rights can be made part of a broader project of democratisation and the formulation of a popular alternative to neo-liberalism. By appropriating an identity which is a product of a colonial situation, Mexico's Etnias can make their collective voice a more powerful one, nationally and internationally, but there is a price to be paid. For the majority of Mexico's growing army of deracinated urban poor, the general class opposition between 'ricos' and 'pobres' has greatest salience to their conditions of life, and is reflected in at least some moments of their quotidian discourse.

The problem is that it is subject to a high degree of interference by other mediations, amongst which may be counted the discourse of identity itself. As Rouse argues, state-sponsored.

> 'Ethnic pluralism' and the assumption that prejudice and disenfranchisement should be combated by the self-mobilising struggles of what are conceived as the homogeneous and horizontal collectivities which suffer from these problems, could be seen as aspects of a reworked hegemonic project of bourgeois-dominated ruling blocs in the era of 'flexible accumulation'.

It is, nevertheless, ironic, as Brown points out, that, in a post-colonial epoch in which 'modern liberal states fully realize their secularism' and 'the mantle of abstract personhood is formally tendered to a whole panoply of those historically excluded from it by humanism's privileging of a single race, gender and organization of sexuality'. The marginalized reject the rubric of humanist inclusion and turn, at least in part, against its very premises. Refusing to be marginalized, to render the differences inconsequential, to be depoliticized as 'lifestyles', 'diversity' or 'persons like any other', we have lately reformulated our historical exclusion as a matter of historically produced and politically rich alterity.

As such politicised identities are therefore both 'a production and contestation of the political terms of liberalism, disciplinary-bureaucratic regimes [and] certain forces of global capitalism'. But we still need to ask how basing claims to recognition on identity can avoid re-subjugating actors historically subjugated through identity; what kinds of politicisation, in what kinds of political context, could sustain subversion of the power structures producing such subjugation? Liberal political definitions of collective Identity through categorical equivalence can be just as 'individualisations their foundations as the more obvious-individualism' of the culture of consumerism promoted by the capitalist corporation.

The possibilities of the dominant bloc in Mexico using the current struggle for 'indigenous autonomy' as a means of fragmenting a broader potential coalition of forces against the current model of capitalist development are apparent. This was not, however, the way that the EZLN began its insurgency against the government of Carlos Salinas de Gortari, on the day of the implementation of the North American Free Trade Agreement.

The Mexican 'proletariat', and particularly a proletariat formed from the 'working poor' is not defunct, and the possibilities of forming broader cross-cutting popular coalitions were demonstrated by the large marches organised in Mexico City in the later months of 1995 by sacked bus-drivers and mechanics from the militant SUTAUR (Sindicato Unico de Trabajadores de Auto-Transporte Urbano-Ruta 100) union, street-sellers displaced from the city centre by riot police, indigenous and mestizo peasants belonging to rural organisations linked to radical urban groups, a variety of public sector manual workers and school teachers etc.

In a city in which 3% of the population forms an upper class which continues to enjoy its privileges in fortified suburbs patrolled by private security guards, and the 20%

who form the middle class have good reasons to believe that the neo-liberal model is not working for them, the formation of multi-class coalitions demanding redistributive policies, and perhaps even a transformation of social property relations, might not be an impossible dream.

In the polls, however, most of the middle classes are opting for the National Action Party, which embodies the strongest of commitments to possessive individualism. The centre-left Party of the Democratic Revolution is increasingly limited to the support of the poorest and most marginalised, including the indigenous rural communities of the states where the direct influence of the EZLN has been less significant than in Chiapas. And a large proportion of the lower classes are simply not voting at all. The struggle for electoral democracy and decency in public life does not, therefore, run parallel to the struggle for greater socioeconomic justice.

Now, we will provide a vivid account of human rights in different cultural contexts.

3

Human Rights and World Culture

"It is of very little use in trying to be dignified, if dignity is no part of your character."

—*Christian Nevell Bovee*

In the present chapter we will describe human rights in different cultural contexts, taking instances of China, African and Islamic societies. Other pertinent issues are also given an elaborate treatment.

Cultural Context of Human Rights in China

In China community and obligation have come traditionally before individual right. In the five basic social relations of Confucian teaching - those between ruler and subjects, parents and children, husband and wife, elder and younger brother, and friend and friend - the connection is one of mutual obligation rather than of reciprocal rights and duties. And in all the pairings, except perhaps the last, the nature of the relationship is hierarchical rather than egalitarian, suggesting unequal duties rather than equal rights. The idea of a right was approximated in the Chinese language by the combination of the word for 'power' with that for 'interest'. But it may be argued that this artificial addition to the language did not change the more organic Chinese conception of law as fulfilling the function of the maintenance of social harmony, which contrasts with the western model of law as arbitration between claims.

And the conception of it in terms of its function in a wider system continues to inform the theory and practice of law in contemporary China. The theory is now Marxist, not Confucian. And law is thought of as an instrument of the policy of the state rather than, as in the West, an 'objective body of authoritative rules'.

Human rights, it follows, should be analysed in this light. As the 'natural rights of man', according to Chinese Marxist theory, they had been a powerful ideological weapon of the rising bourgeoisie; and latterly, as human rights, they have been used by the imperialists, the risen bourgeoisie, to slander measures effected under the dictatorship of the proletariat, such as the suppression of counter-revolutionaries. The proletariat, the argument continues, should recognize that human rights had once fulfilled a progressive function, and that the human rights provisions in the United Nations Charter still had an anti-fascist progressive significance.

But they should also insist on the realization of communist goals beyond bourgeois rights: the dictatorship of the proletariat, the elimination of private ownership, the emancipation of all mankind. In this regard there were more accurate Marxist formulations than those provided by the language of human rights, and all rights were restricted by certain material conditions and cultural levels.

The concept of man, Mao said, lacks content; it lacks the specificity of male and female, adult and child, Chinese and foreign, revolutionary and counter-revolutionary. The only thing left *is* the vague features differentiating man from beast. China has been very cautious in expressing its attitude towards the human rights issues which confront it by virtue of its full membership in the international community of the United Nations. There has been a reluctance to participate in the work of the UN Commission on Human Rights, and a failure to ratify the vast majority of the multilateral treaties on human rights which have been concluded under UN auspices. China's preference is to campaign against imperialism, hegemonism, colonialism and racialism, and to speak not of the rights of man but of those of nations to independence, of races to equal treatment, and of states to development. These are collective rights, not those of individuals, and they impose duties on the currently privileged towards the world's deprived. Human rights should be used as an instrument in the greatest of contemporary struggles for equality among states. Individuals come last, by a distance longer than in African doctrine. Indeed, there is some doubt about whether they come anywhere at all.

For the Chinese render the western (albeit heretical) theory that individuals are constituted subjects of international law - by virtue of the attention paid to human rights in that body of rules - as just another variety of imperialism, a pretext for intervening in the internal affairs of the socialist states.

And the attention paid to the rights of individuals in the Chinese constitution itself is apparently nullified by the article which reads: 'The fundamental rights and duties of citizens are to support the leadership of the Communist Party of China, support the Socialist system and abide by the Constitution and the laws of the People's Republic of China.

Cultural Context of Human Rights in Africa

Remarkably, the Banjul Charter on Human and People's Rights, passed in June 1981 at the eighteenth assembly of heads of state and government of the Organization of African Unity (OAU) devotes its first eighteen articles to the rights of individuals, and only its second eight to the rights of peoples. But it is the idea that the rights of collectivities such as 'peoples' should enjoy at least equal dignity with those of individuals that is often said to be characteristic of African approaches to human rights; and this is reflected in the title of the Banjul Charter.

And if priority is to be determined between individual and collective rights, there is a tendency among the interpreters of traditional African culture to find in favour of the latter. Social harmony, it is said, the preservation of the fabric of social life, comes first in African thought, and the threads in this fabric are either the connections among extended families, or other connections modelled upon them. Individuals are not visible in the fabric, only the duties they discharge, the functions they fulfil. To be a person, in traditional African society, is to be incorporated in this way into a group. Personhood, in contrast to individualism in the West, is intelligible only in the group and not against it. If group values predominate, the language of duty is a more natural usage than that of rights: obligation to the community rather than freedom from it.

This too is reflected in the Banjul Charter, which includes a chapter on duties as well as one on rights. And the duties involve not just the recognition of the equal rights of others, but also the promotion of such substantive goals as the harmonious development of the family (Article 29(1)), national solidarity and independence (Article 294) and

(5)), and African cultural values and unity (Article 29(7) and (8).

Notably, the emphasis on the group, and on duties, connects up to a third strand of African thought which has society organized to meet basic human needs, rather than being the means for the promotion of individual acquisitiveness. Thus traditional African cultures are said to have paid attention to justice in the distribution of social goods in a way that western liberal capitalism has not. This also is reflected in the Banjul Charter, at least in its declaration that fortune, *as* well as race, ethnic group, colour, sex, language, religion, opinion, social origin, birth and status, should be no bar to the enjoyment of the rights and freedoms it guarantees (Article 2).

In addition, there is the assertion in the preamble that it is essential to pay particular attention to the right to development, and that the satisfaction or economic, social and cultural rights is a guarantee for the enjoyment of civil and political rights. Regarding the establishment of hierarchies of human rights, it might be argued that the tendency of African thought is to turn the western list upside down.

Collective rights are first in importance, second come economic and social rights, and third civil and political rights. It is possible to observe this asserted hierarchy at work in contemporary international politics in the goals which African statesmen have set themselves.

Thus, in the first place, when All Mazrui, in his well-known book, expounded an Afro-Asian, but especially an African, view of the United Nations Charter as a global bill of rights, and opposed it to the great powers view of the Charter as a minimalist arrangement for the maintenance of international peace and security, the rights he had in mind were the collective rights to national and racial self-determination. And the international community represented in the United Nations General Assembly endorsed these rights in such instruments as the Declaration on the Granting of Independence to Colonial Countries and Peoples (1960), and the International Convention on the Elimination of All Forms of Racial Discrimination (1966).

Then, secondly, formal independence for the most part having been achieved, there is the mounting preoccupation with the economic and social right to development, which is reflected in the wider international community in such instruments as the Declaration on Permanent Sovereignty over Natural Resources (1966), and more recently the Charter of Economic Rights and Duties of States (1974).

Finally, and most recently, there has been the recognition that, in spite of the importance of the principle of non-intervention in the operation of the OAU, it was wrong for African states to condemn human rights violations in southern Africa and yet remain silent about shortcomings in this regard elsewhere in the continent. The Banjul Charter sprang partly from the crossing of this threshold. And, in it, there is the endorsement of individual rights, as well as of the collective and economic and social rights against which, it has been argued, they have to be judged.

Cultural Context of Human Rights in Islam

In Islam, too, the community the religious community of Muslims, comes before the individual. The Muslim community is a compact wall whose bricks support each other. And the wall must stand on its own without any external buttress. The part of the individual in this community is not merely to act so as to ensure its preservation, but also to recognize that it is the community that-provides for the integration of human personality realized for the good of the collectivity. So in Islam, also, the language of duty seems more natural than that of rights, and obligation is consolidated by its being owed to God. Rules of conduct for all Muslims were laid down by Allah, and communicated through Muhammad, and Muslims do service to God through obedience to these rules.

In fact, the fundamental nature of the idea of obedience to God in Islam shapes the discussion of Islam and human rights so profoundly that rights always seem to be pulled back in the direction of duties. Thus the assertion that the 'essential characteristic of human rights in Islam is that they constitute obligations connected with the Divine and derive their force from this connection. Thus, also, the reluctance to make a stronger claim for human rights in Islam than that they are the privilege of God, in whom all authority ultimately resides. If rights are thought of as freedoms, then - to revert to the distinction made between positive and negative rights - Islam favours 'freedom to' over 'freedom against', freedom to be or to become over freedom from external constraint.

True freedom consists in surrendering to the Divine will rather than in some artificial separation from the community of God. And while it was possible for God's representative on earth, the caliph, to act unjustly, this did not confer on his subjects a right of resistance. In this regard, there has been in Islamic doctrine no 'protestant' revolution of the kind we paid attention to. Rights remain subordinate to and determined by duties. And, if there are difficulties about the autonomy of rights in Islam, there is a question too about whether they are human in the sense of being applicable to all human beings.

Human rights in Islam, it has been said, are the privileges only of a person of full legal capacity - 'a living human being of mature age, free, and of Moslem faith. Some arrangement might be made for non-Muslims residing in Muslim lands provided they paid the poll-tax, but the rights that were guaranteed in exchange for this - to security of life and property, and freedom of prayer' - did not derive from a notion that all humans had rights in virtue of their humanity, but from the need to make practical arrangements for those not of the faith. And, in any event, the freedom of prayer did not extend to Muslims.

Religious liberty meant the freedom of non-Muslims to practise their religion unobtrusively in Muslim lands, or to abandon it in favour of Islam. There could be no traffic the other way, for Islam had transcended other religious systems. Like Christianity, Islam approached the notion, prerequisite to the emergence of the idea of human rights, that there was a unity in mankind which made no difference between an Arab and a non-Arab, a white man and *a* black man. St. Paul in its doctrine stated that in Christ there was to be neither Jew nor Greek, it was the faith that made the difference. The brotherhood of man was for every believer in Islam, just as it was for every believer in Christ.

The important contrast between the two religions in regard to their attitude to human rights lay elsewhere. The unworldly strand of Christian thought which had all men equal in the sight of God, and in the world to come, allowed Christian doctrine to detach itself from a particular sovereign, and eventually to give place to the theory of natural rights which saw value in every individual regardless of religious attachment. Islam, not making any distinction between Caesar's and God's, for all was God's, did not allow a theory of religious duty to turn into one of political right. The past few decades have witnessed the inexorable rise of the application of international human rights law as well as the extension of a wider public discourse on human rights, to the point where human rights could be seen as one of the most globalised political values of our times. The language of liberal human rights has moved in to fill the vacuum left by the demise of grand political narratives in the aftermath of the Cold War. Notwithstanding disputes over their conceptualisation and application, human rights are among the few Utopian ideals left, and there is still a remarkable degree of consensus by governments on the principle at least that certain rights be protected under international law. Historically, anthropological perspectives on transnational processes have been hampered by two related factors: (1) a methodological emphasis on localism; and (2) a theoretical concern with 'culture'. Anthropology's prolonged love affair with local culture has meant that at various junctures, anthropologists have positioned themselves in critical opposition to universal values and transnational such as 'human rights'.

The canonical post-Second World statement shaping the response of a generation was made by Melville Herskovits, the author of the American Anthropological Association (AAA) executive board's statement on human rights in 1947. The relativism of Herskovits and others in the Boasian tradition shone through their critique of what they perceived as the ethnocentric extension of absolutist Western values. Herskovits exhorted the emergent world order to respect cultural differences, and raised 'culture' to the level of a supreme ethical value. In this position of radical cultural relativism, as Jack Donnelly comments, culture is the sole source of the validity of a moral right or rule. Particular cultural values, so it follows, should under no conditions be supplanted by universal moral values, for example, conceptions of human rights. In his reference to 'underlying cultural values', Herskovits hoped to play anthropology's trump card in order to reassert the continued usefulness of the discipline. In so doing, he defined the role of anthropologists as advocates of indigenous peoples who would defend them from attempts by international agencies such as the UN to globalise a set of 'Western' moral values.

He also sought to enshrine the unique capacity of the anthropologist to construct a holistic version of each society's inner cultural logic. Herskovits's position has been subjected to a number of critiques but its most serious flaw lies in a rather hopeful belief in the essential moral rectitude contained within 'culture'. Herskovits was saying that even if the political system is abusive, cultural values (as opposed to say, political values?) could -be invoked to restore a balanced social order. Such rose-tinted optimism was particularly inappropriate so soon after the Second World War and the Nazi Holocaust, and left unexplained why 'underlying cultural values' in Germany during the Third Reich did not check Nazi hegemony.

Obviously, Herskovits was not willing to consider the possibility that certain values might actively promote cruel and inhumane practices, or, more specifically with regard to the constellation of 'cultural values' around anti-semitism in modern Europe, mass genocide. Because of anthropologists' exalting of culture, and enduring fascination with the more unfamiliar and seemingly bizarre characteristics of the non-Western other (encountered in symbolism, ritual and forms of representation generally), some human rights theorists have lambasted anthropology as the last bastion of cultural absolutism, and anthropologists as surveyors of exotica.

For instance, Rhoda Howard rhetorically charges that: 'Anthropological conclusions both about the substance of cultural values and about the integrative, unchanging nature of cultural norms are drawn from highly questionable data that reflect both the arrogance and the romanticism of Western observers. This is all part of Howard's project to reject the position of 'romantic communitarianism' (shared by a rogue's gallery of anthropologists, communists and fascists) and reassert a liberal individualistic conception of human rights. Howard over-homogenises the variety of perspectives within anthropology and she operates with an anachronistic vision of how anthropologists deal with 'tradition'. Yet some aspects of her critique are warranted, in that more than any other discipline, anthropology has contributed to culturalist, constructivist and communitarian conceptions of society (though only marginally more so than Howard's own intellectual bolt-hole, sociology).

At present, discussions of the cross-cultural applicability of human rights still revolve around the universalism / relativism debate and the importance of culture. Both universalism and relativism have something to recommend themselves to the ethnographer; universalism makes comparison possible, and yet relativism grants precedence to immediate contexts and engenders a sensitivity to diversity.

Yet as with most absolutist dualisms, the universalist/ relativist polarity is too totalising in its conceptualisation. The intellectual efforts of those seeking to develop a framework for understanding the social life of rights would be better directed not towards foreclosing their ontological status, but instead by exploring their meaning and use. What is needed are more detailed studies of human rights according to the actions and intentions of social actors, within wider historical constraints of institutionalised power.

Cultural Relativist Critique

The inability of philosophers and social and legal theorists to agree on the moral foundations of human rights is perhaps the most immediate factor in the relativists' favour. This fact greatly strengthens the hand of moral pluralists such as Steven Lukes (1991) who has challenged the efforts of writers such as Habermas, Kant and Rawls to establish an 'Archimedean point' which would provide universal rational foundations for generalisable norms and categories of justice.

All approaches broadly within the cultural relativist tradition point towards the historically and culturally bounded nature of human rights discourses, and therefore to their socially constructed nature. According to relativists, human rights are inseparable from the mentality of the Enlightenment, and as presently construed are the product of a particular society at a particular time.

The Universal Declaration of Human Rights made in 1948 is therefore universal only in pretension, not in practice, since it is a Charter of an idealist European political philosophy. Many forms of relativism begin with a critique of universalists' conceptions of 'human nature'. Within the rationalist tradition, human rights presuppose a stable (and usually Hobbesian) conception of human nature which includes a unified subject with a knowable essence and basic needs.

Having established the nature of a universal human ontology, objectivity can be claimed for value judgements about political, economic and legal arrangements. The construction of 'human nature' was put to direct political usage by those such as John Locke and Immanuel Kant to uphold their versions of the social contract and therefore to limit the absolute rights of monarchs. A more recent and influential conception of human nature /rights is found in the work of the sociologist Bryan S. Turner (1993), which incorporates elements of relativism, with the aim of creating a more flexible and globally applicable conception of human rights.

Turner rejects the rationalist and individualist elements in Kant's philosophy, since they do not allow for a moral community to be built upon sympathy and emotive criteria. Turner argues that a conception of human ontology is a precondition for any notion of human rights and he invokes the 'philosophical anthropology' of Arnold Gehlen and Helmut Plessner. According to this view, humans are characterised by their 'world-openness' and relative lack of instincts. In contrast to the Hobbesian version of history, social institutions are needed because humans are physically and ontologically frail and 'unfinished', not because they are aggressive and bent on domination.

Social institutions and social arrangements are precarious, so social relations are characterised by risk and instability. Whereas human happiness is noted for its variety, human misery is relatively uniform, leading to a notion of human frailty as the universal feature of human existence. For most anthropologists, the category of human nature is one of the more offensive ways of imposing the prejudices of 'Western culture'.

In the AAA statement, much of Herskovits's argument rested on the principle that the individual's personality is shaped by his/her culture. The first proposition which

Herskovits deemed essential in any 'Bill of Human Rights' stated, 'The individual realizes his personality through his culture, hence respect for individual differences entails a respect for cultural differences. Here, 'culture' and 'cultural differences' are deployed to deconstruct the universal rational individual of classical political economy upon which human rights discourses depend. As part of a general anti-essentialism, relativists reject the notion of a unified subject with a knowable essence, whether it be frail or domineering.

There can be no essential characteristics of human nature or human rights, which exist outside of discourse, history, context or agency. A relativist critique of Bryan Turner's formulation of a 'frail' human nature would say that Turner is advancing an inherently paradoxical claim that it is our lack of essence which is universally human. The concept of frailty may-be open to a certain degree of relativisation since it constructs human nature in the weakest possible terms without abandoning the idea altogether, but it ultimately does not escape from problems which arise from attempts to classify through demarcated definitional boundaries based upon particular shared (manifest or latent) commonalities. Existence must precede essence for relativism to be possible, and the aspect of existence which most challenges any universal essence is 'culture'.

If 'human nature' presupposes a conception of 'human being', then there is an immediate difficulty of translation in that some cultures may not have such a concept at all. American Indian languages such as those of the Navajo and Hopi construct humanness as belonging solely to those within the boundaries of the community, whose collective name means 'the people'.

Outsiders are perceived to be non-human to a certain

degree, particularly in origin myths. Even if there is a conception of 'human being' within a language and culture, universal notions of rights or duties may not be necessarily derived from it. Dignity may not be universally human at all, but may be distributed unevenly by a system of social stratification, as in the Hindu caste system. Anthropological critiques of human nature, being based on the socially constructed nature of the 'person', inherently imply a rejection of the category 'individual' which is fundamental to human rights law. Relativists point out that as it is presently constituted, international human rights law is fundamentally grounded in individual rights, and therefore remains unable to flexibly respond to a global diversity of legal systems.

The UN is still uncomfortable with less individualist conceptions of rights in its application of human rights procedures. It operates with what Richard Falk calls a 'normative blindness towards indigenous peoples', who may claim communal rights to land ownership or political self determination. The critique of rights as an ideology of Western individualism and liberalism has a long pedigree.

Marx (1977) noted long ago that eighteenth-century European notions of rights are predicated to a large degree on bourgeois categories of possessive individualism and the free market. According to some relativists, moral status belongs more to collective entities than to individuals. In their conception and application, then, human rights are an ethnocentric extension of European concepts of individualistic rights to societies with more communalistic political traditions.

The implication here parallels that of the AAA statement on human rights: that outsiders should not interfere in moral issues which are internal to another culture, since this would usually lead to the arbitrary silencing of collectivist narratives by 'Western' individualist ones. In arguing for empirical basis for human rights, Alison Dundes Renteln (1985, 1988, 1990), accepts cultural relativist descriptions of the world as made up of different societies with divergent moral value systems, but rejects the prescription of tolerance which conventionally results from such portrayals. This seemingly contradictory argument merits close attention.

Renteln (1988) argues that 'Relativism is compatible with cross-cultural universals' and she has elaborated an approach which grounds its universalism empirically.

Unlike the political philosophers entering into this debate, her theoretical discussion of the universalism/ relativism issue is combined with a cross-cultural survey of moral values. She claims that human rights as such do not exist empirically, and that there is remarkable diversity in notions of justice and morality. For instance, neither freedom of speech nor freedom of religious practice seem particularly entrenched, and the death penalty is enforced in different contexts for an enormous range of different offences - from adultery to witchcraft to blasphemy.

Renteln concludes that there is only one ubiquitous moral principle and that is, 'retribution tied to proportionality'- that the punishment is proportional to the gravity of the crime. One expression of this principle is lex talionis, or in the Old Testament, 'an eye for an eye, etc.'. Renteln's ultimate objective is to build human rights standards which have a legitimacy across the globe. These values would be grounded not in Western theories of natural rights, but on the empirically proven universality of a moral principle of reciprocal vengeance. Renteln believes that the principle of negative reciprocity limits violence and encourages stability, but anyone remotely familiar with the history of over 25 years of revenge killings in Northern Ireland is aware that lex tationis can incite, escalate and perpetuate violence as much as restrain it. Furthermore, any logical move from prevalence to moral rightness is obviously problematic, and Renteln makes a naive conflation of what is common and what is morally justifiable. Renteln (1990) advocates ethnography, but her own study indulges in Frazerian sweeps of the globe, effacing the attitudes, perceptions and practices invoked in local struggles over rights.

In her urge to present the global evidence for a single value which supposedly underpins human rights standards, Renteln highlights the richness of ethnographic accounts. Perhaps more importantly, Renteln is caught on the horns of her own contradictory stance: that is, she is a relativist who asserts the ethnocentric nature of any value judgements, yet she wants to build a universal conception of human rights through an empirical survey of local forms of justice.

Limitations of Cultural Relativism

Relativism does have merits when thinking about the possible methods of a social inquiry into rights. For ethnographers of human rights, the most valuable critique of universalist perspectives is that they provide little or no framework for studying rights 'on the ground'.

In defending conceptions of human nature, and arguing that universal rights must be designated through an overarching super-perspective, rationalist social philosophy and natural law lift the discussion of rights out of any particular context and raise it to the level of the categorical imperative. Practical reason is swept away by a formalistic analysis of a priori synthetic principles, and human actions are continually related to absolute maxims and 'natural' law. In particular, the influence of the neo-Kantian tradition in human rights theory has led to too great an emphasis on securing a priori foundations and continues to obstruct empirical attempts to understand rights. Despite its methodological insights, cultural relativism suffers from a number of delusions and limitations. As many have noted, it undermines its own truth claims and it implies moral nihilism (Gellner 1982; Jarvie 1984).

That is, relativism generates a meta-narrative with totalising claims at the same time as generating a self-undermining critique of the very possibility of meta-narratives and totalising claims. Accusations of moral nihilism are perhaps easier for relativists to defend; Richard Rorty (1993) makes an impassioned plea for the continued value of doing human rights, yet he justifies such actions in the contingent present rather than by appealing to a-temporal universals.

Yet one can only construct a very weak defence of actions by relying on emotions and courage alone, and eschewing all recourse to rational forms of argumentation. Rights without a meta-narrative are like a car without seat-belts; on hitting the first moral bump with ontological implications, the passengers' safety is jeopardised. Ironically, the emphasis on conventions by social constructionists such as Rorty means that their position ends up sharing many attributes with utilitarianism and legal positivism in so far as they too are founded upon convention and precedent, the open recognition of which would surely horrify most postmodernists.

Yet the most serious contingent 'reality' is that-relativism itself is an integral part of the meta-narrative of those governments who actively oppose the applications of international human rights to their polities. The tolerance of relativism here has a directly conservative political implication - the maintenance of highly inegalitarian and repressive political systems.

An undeniable truth is that many governments around the world continue to carry out abominable acts against 'their' populations, and relativism is the most useful available ideology which facilitates international acquiescence in state repression. Cultural relativism provides an inaccurate set of descriptions of moral pluralism since it wields a misguided conception of culture. Relativist rights theorists such as Ronald Dworkin (1977) seem quite unaware of the recent discussions of 'culture' in the social sciences and humanities which have sought to de-reify this concept and so deprive it of its ontological security.

Instead, the various relativisms totalise and reify 'culture', constructing it as internally uniform and hermetically bounded. 'Culture' is seen as shared and normative, not as cross-cut by social differences (age, caste, gender, etc.), or characterised as contested, fragmented, contextualised and emergent. Culture is referred to as an entity, not as a process; as a noun, not a verb. For their doctrine to be coherent, cultural relativists seem to hold a nineteenth-century notion of culture as discrete and homogeneous, as the product of isolation, and as the basis of all difference and similarity between human beings. Their relativism is predicated upon bounded conceptions of linguistic and cultural systems, but it falls apart in contexts of hybridity, creolisation, intermixture and the overlapping of political traditions. Just as earlier Boasian relativisms ignored global realities such as colonialism, attempts at undermining human rights by reference to 'culture' have ignored transnational juridical processes.

Despite the charges of some governments of 'cultural imperialism' in the application of international law, human rights doctrine has been adopted by many people to whom it was once foreign.

For instance, Mayan human rights organisations in Guatemala reproduce international human rights law faithfully, and only invoke *'la cultura'* to reinforce universal conceptions of needs." Groups who now refer to themselves as 'indigenous peoples' are aware of human rights discourses, if only because they have experienced state violence and marginalisation from national political processes. Indigenous peoples in contexts are different as Panama, Canada and South Africa are engaging in close negotiations with their governments over their constitutional claims for linguistic and territorial rights and political sovereignty. It is simply not possible now to live anywhere without regular encounters with agents or institutions of the nation-state, as it was during the heyday of anthropological functionalism and cultural relativism in the early to mid-twentieth century. A lack of participation in state institutions and an awareness of a lowly status position in national society is now as indicative of 'indigenous' status as it was of 'peasant' status when Wolf defined it in the 1950s.

This is paralleled by an awareness on the part of many indigenous peoples of international institutions and of their greater possibilities for participation in them compared to national institutions. Increasingly, indigenous peoples actively seek representation at international fora, and attend such bodies with legal advisers in tow. Indeed, the whole concept of 'indigenous peoples' is now inseparable from human rights discourses which represent them as victims of abusive governments. It is no coincidence that the activities around the UN Year of Indigenous Peoples in

1993 came under the UN's human rights budget line, just as it is no coincidence that they represented less than 1 per cent of that budget.

Now, we will discuss human rights from sociological viewpoint. The text is intends to provide authoritative information.

4

Sociological Route to Human Rights

> "Disappointment to a nobel soul is what cold water is to burning metal: it strengthens, tempers, intensifies, but never destroys it."
>
> —*Eliza Tabor*

Human rights from sociological angle is described in the present chapter. Instances are cited to substantiate the text.

The official doctrine underlying the international law of human rights, whatever its stage of development and however many the signatories of its covenants, is that it is in principle universal. It does not suggest (except where special regional arrangements have been made, which must then not conflict with general international law) that there are different rules for Africans, and Chinese, and Muslims. The interpretation of human rights varies with culture both as to their place in society and as to the hierarchy established among them. And there may even be doubt about whether some societies pay any serious attention to human rights at all - preferring citizen to human and duty to right.

Here three purported solutions to the problem of bringing

the universal and the particular together are tried and mentioned below.

1. Human Rights as Particular Rights

First suggested solution to the problem of asserting universal human rights in a culturally plural world was to treat the expression 'human rights' as one that, all or most societies recognize, but which they define in terms of the values of their particular society. To be human is to be Javanese. The enjoyment of human rights might result only from participation in a real community, and not from some abstract connection to human society as a whole. Human rights list variety not similarity. Java is different from Ghana, and there is no basis for preferring Javanese conceptions of human rights to Ghanaian ones. The idea that conceptions of rights vary according to culture is an anthropological commonplace.

If it were not true, doing anthropology would lose much of its point. It might seem, then, an attractive solution to allow human rights to take on whatever is the local colour. But this is not a resolution of our difficulty. It is a surrender to the universality of particularism.

2. Human Rights as 'core' Rights

The second proposed solution has the merit of confronting this question directly. It asks whether there is in fact a core of basic rights that is common to all cultures despite their apparently divergent theories. This question is consistent with the natural rights tradition. If there are rights whose content can be decided upon by the use of right reason, then since reason is a human faculty the outcome of the process of decision-making should be similar across cultures. The modern investigation of this proposition might take a natural scientific form as in the inquiry into the biological basis of morality.

Or it might be based on some sociological hypothesis like Barrington Moore's notion of the unity of human misery, according to which general opposition to human suffering is a standpoint that transcends differences of place and time. Or it might be based more on the refinement of inductive generalizations, as in the concern to 'distill from the multiplicity of philosophies and ideologies and their divergent values any universals that may exist'. What these investigations might be expected to produce, if anything, is a lowest common denominator of basic or core rights, which, if found across all societies, would then have a proper positive claim to the label 'human rights'. There are difficulties with the historical quality of this mode of inquiry, and also with its wishful character - suggesting that anyone determined to find (or not to find) similarities across cultures will shape the evidence to fit the thesis. But its cross-cultural perspective has given rise to some progressive features in the investigation of human rights in world politics of which we may mention three.

The first is the disposition to become aware of and make explicit our own value preferences and implicit comparisons in thinking about human rights abroad. The second is the attempt to marshal data that might begin to reveal global patterns in regard to conceptions of rights, their observancc, and their enforcement. The third has to do with measurement: of 'human rights conditions' in general (establishing an index that would reflect all the values in the Universal Declaration); or of performance on particular rights (economic and social rights as approximated, for example, by the Physical Quality of Life Index, and civil and political rights as judged, for example, by Freedom House).

Although it may be a surprise to some of their authors, all of these approaches can be placed in a natural rights tradition - at least to the extent that they do not suppose that cultural relativity disposes of the cross-cultural enterprise from the outset. There is also an inverted form of our second solution which we might notice here. It seeks universal human rights, not in the pursuit of what is common to all cultures, but in the production of a list which takes something from all cultures. According to this notion, human rights that *were* properly universal would do something for Islam, and for China, and for Africa and so on, rather than relying on the straightforward conversion of western into universal values.

In fact, the difficulty with this procedure is that while it might reduce the ethnocentrism of declarations about them, it abandons in the process any notion of universal rights. Drawing up a long list to satisfy everybody merely adds variety together. It does nothing to resolve the differences between one item or group of items on the list and another, and it would invite particular societies to consult only their section of the document. It therefore makes no progress beyond our first solution, which had human rights as particular rights. And if a resolution among items were attempted, or an effort made to produce a list that was common to all societies, only an outcome that was reasonable, and not merely the arbitrary product of some political bargain, would deserve recognition.

3. Human Rights in the Global Cosmopolitan Culture

Simultaneously, the third proposed solution to the problem of establishing that there are universal human rights was that there exists in the contemporary world a single cosmopolitan culture which is spread across all indigenous cultures, and which carries to each of them what are, in some at least geographical sense, global human rights. This is the common culture of modernity which has touched, some would argue that it has engulfed, all societies in virtue of the rise of a global economy.

States, regions, cities, families, patterns of life, are all shaped by this culture. All over the world individuals have been pulled away by its operation from their traditional attachment to the local community. In these circumstances, the philosophy of human rights can be rendered as the natural response to changing conditions, a logical and necessary evolution of the means for realizing human dignity. Human rights are part of a world social process, the institutional expression of which is the international law of human rights that we considered above.

And if international law is, as we suggested earlier, in some degree an inter-cultural law as well, we may appeal to it as evidence for the existence of universal standards of human rights.

Notably, there are at least three difficulties with this association of human rights with the emerging common culture of modernity.

1. The first is that there is not one single animal called the 'common culture of modernity'. The process of modernization might be said to produce two cultures, as in the centre-periphery model of it and the idea that it creates a dual economy in developing societies. Or it might be said to produce as many cultures as there are societies, modernization affecting each differently. Or, with particular reference to how human rights are viewed, it might - to adopt Professor Macpherson's scheme - be reduced to three political models based on dominant conceptions of democracy

- the liberal-democratic, the communist, and that in the underdeveloped world.

Civil and political rights are associated with the first conception; economic and social rights with the second; and collective rights with the third. No one of these is preferable to the others. They simply reflect different priorities in different material circumstances.

2. The second difficulty follows from the first. If there is more than one culture associated with the process of modernization, then there is no basis for an appeal to that process itself to settle an argument about universal human rights. Calling up the international law of human rights as evidence for the existence of a world cosmopolitan culture of which all societies are part, and whose rules should then apply to them, fails because international law itself is subject to interpretation from the standpoint of this or that culture.

The argument that takes place between East and West, and also between North and South, on the question of human rights, does show some point in Macpherson's distinction between three worlds of democracy.

3. A third objection to the idea of a common culture of modernity questions not its existence but its pedigree. A common culture does in some degree exist in the contemporary world, but the extent of it is the measure of westernization and not of modernization. It is a species of imperialism, a charge the West seeks to avoid by calling it a world social process, or modernization, or an emerging global social structure. On the matter of human rights in particular, the West employs a similar dodge.

What is called the international law of human rights,

a seemingly neutral title, is in fact the machine for widening and deepening the legitimacy of western conceptions of the good society. As a result, according to this view, Third World conceptions of human rights must be presented as different conceptions if they are to play any part in the strategy for emergence from western dominance.

The first argument was the most radical. In its 'three worlds of democracy' form the separate worlds were constructed of different conceptions of rights that were in principle unassimilable. One might allow successfully either for civil and political liberty, or for economic and social equality, but not at the same time and in the same place for both. The flaw in this objection is that it seems to suggest that the three worlds are sealed off from one another, immune to external criticism. This seems doubtful empirically.

It may be true that the 'three worlds of democracy' accurately convey three main tendencies in the world in the interpretation of human rights, but we can observe these tendencies contesting with each other within western and eastern and southern societies, as well as between the West, the East and the South. Moreover, if we take, with Macpherson, Locke to be the captain of the civil and political rights team, Marx of the economic and social rights team, and Rousseau of the collective rights team these are three great western thinkers invoked in what is now a global contest.

That it is possible to characterize the contemporary debate about human rights in world politics by reference to these western figures itself casts doubt on the disposition to have the tripartite division as the more fundamental reality than the contest which makes the division intelligible. The second difficulty with the argument for universal human rights as part of a common global culture was that this global culture was subject to interpretation by the primary cultural groups, over which the so-called world culture was stretched. Thus the international law of human rights was in reality African, or Chinese, or Islamic, or western, and not some meta-law above the cultures. There is a naive realism about this difficulty. It is tautological that western, or Islamic, or Chinese lawyers interpret international law from a western, or Islamic, or Chinese point of view. It is plainly not true that they regard international law merely as the vehicle for their own cultural freight.

A law among nations acceptable to all its members suggests the existence of some common ground, and not merely the outward thrust of domestic preoccupations. This common ground then has some autonomous existence which it is the burden of international lawyers to explicate. They might disagree about it. But this does not sanction the reductionist view that international law can be understood only at the level of the cultures participating in it. For the disagreement might take place within as well as among cultures. The third difficulty concerned the pedigree of the global cosmopolitan culture. It may be true that the chief fact about modernity is its westernness, and that the international law of human rights, like all international law, is more an export of the West to the rest of the world than of the rest of the world to the West.

It may also be true that the emancipation of the Third World requires the uncovering of authentic indigenous conceptions of 'human rights' with which to confront the notions of the imperialists. Ironically, however, it may be argued that the emergence from western dominance is not advanced by the assertion of the cultural relativity of all values, but rather by appealing to certain universal principles, such as that of state sovereignty, to roll back the hegemony of the imperialists.

And even if the right asserted is a right to be different, it is one protected by a doctrine long familiar in the western world, namely the principle of self-determination. Moreover, if the countries and peoples of the Third World want something positive from the First and Second Worlds in addition to the right to be left alone, there is even more reason to underline the existence of a common moral world in which the weak can make demands on the strong to some point. These arguments show the utility of acting as if a common moral world existed; they do not prove its existence. But what is being suggested here is that the emergence of the new states, and the associated revival of suppressed cultures, has not in fact meant the jettisoning of western doctrine.

What it has meant is, in part, the use of western principles against their authors, and in part the accommodation of a western tradition to these new arrivals. The principle of self-determination may illustrate this process at work. It is a western principle, at least as old as the French Revolution, which the new states used to pin their independence. Since independence they have added racial and economic interpretations to the principle that were not previously associated with it. In this respect, the common cosmopolitan culture has been received and then added to from underneath, not imposed and entrenched from on top.

Relativsm and Naturalism

In fact, the doctrine of cultural relativism asserts that rules about morality vary from place to place. This seems an uncontroversial assertion. But if the general moral prescription drawn from it is that we should adopt in each place the rules of that place, this is clear and helpful only if the boundaries between one place and another are clear. When, as in the contemporary world, the downward seepage of a global cosmopolitan civilization has obscured even further cultural boundaries that were previously hardly clear, this aspect of the doctrine of cultural relativism is misleading if not always chaotic. The same difficulty then applies to our second feature of the doctrine of cultural relativism, which was that the way to understand moral variety was to place it in its cultural context.

There can be no objection to this attempt at understanding, but much debate about the nature and limits of the cultural context. It is the third feature of the doctrine of cultural relativism that is the most distinctive and important from a moral point of view. It is the assertion that moral claims derive from, and are enmeshed in, a cultural context which is itself the source of their validity.

From this strong version of cultural relativism, two things might be said to follow.

The first is that each culture has a pattern of life that is of equal validity to all the others.

The second is that moral claims deriving from outside a culture have no validity within it. The first implication seems logically mistaken, the second morally obnoxious. The moral conclusion to be drawn from Ruth Benedict's assertion that all cultures create equally valid patterns of life is, as Clifford Geertz has pointed out, a strange one. It is that anything one group of people is inclined towards doing is worthy of respect by another. But the mistake of logic takes place prior to the drawing of this conclusion.

Obviously, it is in the assumption that the doctrine of cultural relativism has egalitarian consequences. In logic, the doctrine of cultural relativism cannot rank cultures as equal or unequal. All the doctrine can do is to observe that values are endogenously derived. If the local value is to assert global superiority, that is to say inequality, then no argument from cultural relativism can be mounted against it. The association of cultural relativism with egalitarianism may or may not be empirically demonstrable, but it is not connection that is logically required. As to moral obnoxiousness, to assert that moral claims deriving from outside culture have no validity within it is effectively to withdraw a society from the moral scrutiny of others. The argument that you have to be of us to understand us, and to have a right of criticism, rules out even comment, let alone intervention, on the part of outsiders.

The perfect society would not require criticism either external or internal. But the doctrine of cultural relativism can defend imperfect as well as perfect societies, and these are perhaps of greater moral interest. Should the rest of the world have no say about a society in which the rulers practise slavery or starve their people? If this is what the doctrine of cultural relativism allows, then there is some doubt about whether it should be called a moral doctrine at all. It is certainly not a doctrine that has ever been part of the orthodoxy of international society.

On the contrary, the international legal doctrine of a minimum standard of justice has never allowed the defence of non-intervention for conduct that has 'outraged the conscience of mankind'. So despite its progressive association with the campaign against imperialism, what the doctrine of cultural relativity allows in practice is a surrender to what John Stuart Mill called the 'despotism of custom'. It allows the predominant opinion in any locality to prevail whether or not there is any good reason to support it.

The despotism is more remarkable when arbitrary. As Mill again observed, the person who 'devolves upon his own world the responsibility of being in the right against the dissentient world of other people' is never troubled by the fact that 'mere accident has decided which of the numerous worlds is the object of his reliance, and that the same causes which make him a Churchman in London, would have made him a Buddhist or a Confucian in Peking'. However true it is that we all tend to devolve upon our own worlds the responsibility of being in the right against others, this is not a reason to withdraw from moral argument in world politics altogether.

Otherwise, the argument for human fallibility would beggar every enterprise. At the same time, we have to recognize that conceptions of human rights do vary with culture, and that this is something that has to be taken into account in the making of policy. The problem is to find a balance between insistence on the human rights that everyone ought to enjoy, by virtue of their humanity, and the recognition that the existence, content and importance of these rights is contested. The response suggests that it is the duty of governments (supposing that they act for societies) to act when they are sure (not absolutely certain, which is impossible) of being right, and that it is not conscientiousness but cowardice to shrink from acting on their opinions.

The fact that government has in the past raised bad taxes, and fought unjust wars, is not an argument against taxation, or war when provoked. The procedure Mill offers concerns how to arrive at what is right, and it consists in rectifying mistakes by discussion and experience. The whole value of human judgement, says Mill, is that it can be set right when wrong, and any conduct worthy of respect is that which is exposed to criticism. What is fixed on temporarily as right is the outcome of the collision of opposing opinions. Even what is wholly true must be contested to avoid its becoming a mere prejudice. This procedure does not allow the imposition of a moral truth, or the coercion of those not seized of it, in Mill's view, because coercion is only legitimate for the protection of the self and not for the enlightenment of others.

But it does suggest a view of the discussion of human rights in international politics as appealing to the empire of reason and not merely to that of power, or circumstance. It supposes, more deeply, that no human being can seriously hold some ethical principle to be right, or imperative, without wishing that others too deem it right, or imperative. So we have returned to the single moral universe of the natural rights theorists. It may be argued that this is the only world in which it is possible to make sense of an African, or a Muslim, or a Chinese, or a Western claim about an order of moral priorities. Each of them would have the world as *a* whole adopt its particular priorities. If this were not true of any one of them, there would be no reason for the rest to take it seriously. But each of them at the same time accepts that a rational conversation about rights, Mill's procedure, is worth having. The point put as a point of prudence, has been well expressed in Chinese legal doctrine, in a passage arguing for the reality of international law, and against cultural relativism. The position 'They say they are right, we say we are right,' was detrimental to China's struggle because it would then have no legal right to criticize the infraction of the law by capitalist countries. If the single moral world were not a reality, it would be a good idea to invent it.

Global Privacy

Remarkably, Nancy Fraser points out, Rorty himself has always displayed an unusually strong commitment to culture, and this commitment forces its way into some of the most troubling and contradictory aspects of his own writing. According to Fraser, Rorty's recent thought is structured around a series of collisions between "Romanticism and pragmatism, poetry and politics". Fraser distinguishes three ways in which he tries to reconcile these contradictory impulses toward transgressive aesthetics and toward liberal or reformist politics.

1. The first is the "invisible hand" conception, which asserts that the two are "natural partners," that the "strong poet" and the "reform politician" are "variants of the same species."
2. The second is the "sublimity or decency" conception, which suggests that "one has to choose between the sublime 'cruelty of the strong poet and the beautiful kindness of the political reformer'.
3. The third and most recent is the "partition" position, which declares a truce by allotting to each a separate sphere of influence. "The Romantic impulse will have free rein in what will henceforth be 'the private sector.' But it will not be permitted any political pretensions. Pragmatism, on the other hand, will have exclusive rights to 'the public sector.' But it will be barred from entertaining any notions of radical change that could challenge the 'private' cultural hegemony of Romanticism".

In the light of Fraser's analysis, it seems clear that for Rorty the unforgivable sin of the contemporary academic left is its claim to be political by virtue of its attention to culture. For this claim ignores any need for Rorty's emphatic demarcation between private and public.

It asserts or assumes that the private (culture) *is* already sufficiently public (political). Thus it might seem to return to Rorty's own first position, where aesthetics stood in for pragmatism's own distance from the ideal of objectivity. Fraser describes it (not very sympathetically) as a "Sorelian temptation": admiration for the visionary artist/leader who transgresses social norms, whose actions are revolutionary creations both in aesthetics and in politics. Unfortunately, as Fraser and Rorty seem to agree, this cultural model of politics is both undemocratic and impractical: "to say goodbye to objectivity is not necessarily to say hello to a single, unitary solidarity and ... what's good for poets is not necessarily good for workers, peasants, and the hard-core unemployed".

The question of whether cultural politics is necessarily reducible to these formulations will be addressed later. Rorty's turn against cultural politics is expressed unambiguously in a debate with Andrew Ross in the pages of Dissent. There he sets up an opposition between the real politics of the Old Left, which is electoral politics (drafting and Passing bills) and the merely academic politics of the New Left, which is cultural politics (demands for total social transformation, for change at the deep level language, and so on). Cultural politics can be negatively defined, for Rorty, as politics that doesn't have to do with legislation, with passing bills into laws. "It is true that the Old Left ignored a lot of injustices and inequalities," he writes, -but it is also true that it struggled, with good effect, against a lot of other injustices and inequalities. The utility of this left is illustrated by its role in drafting and passing Lyndon Johnsoifs Great Society bills. The inutility of Ross's left is suggested by its disdainful refusal to think in terms of drafting and passing bills.

In fact, there is no mention of patriotism or nationalism in this argument. If Rorty has no need of the patriotism theme here, it's because the substance of his reproaches against the "unpatriotic" academy is already contained in his reproaches against those who make claims for cultural politics. In other words, for Rorty, too little attachment to the nation produces the same undesirable effects as too great an attachment to culture. The two sins are mysteriously and suspiciously interchangeable. But something must be wrong if two such unlike adjectives as cultural and unpatriotic are made to function as equivalents. And something is indeed wrong. For if we extract the national/international problematic from the argumentative bile of "The Unpatriotic Academy," dust it off, and carefully insert it back into Rorty's argument against cultural politics, it turns out to lead somewhere very different. Let us translate Rorty's opposition between law and culture, the first real and public, the second unreal and private, from the national to the international scale. In the absence of a world government, human rights instruments are of course not international law in the strict national sense; they are usually referred to as "soft" law.

But they are certainly public in the ordinary meanings of that term, which is to say objects that invite widespread discussion and demand universal application. Hence we would seem to get a parallel opposition between human rights internationalism, on the one hand, based on the universality of the law, and on the other hand a sort of cultural cosmopolitanism based on respect for the unique particularity of different cultures. On the cultural particularity side we would find only those privileged academic elites whom Rorty describes, in a killing association with aestheticism, as "connoisseurs of diversity".

On the legal universality side we would find a solid majority of popular opinion. Given the opposition between real politics and cultural politics on which he so fiercely insists, one would expect Rorty to rejoice that human rights, like domestic legislation, are backed by an extensive democratic sense of fairness and decency. One would expect him to prefer human rights to culture's vanguardist appreciation of diversity and aesthetic skepticism about norms. And one would thus expect him to argue that human rights represent just the right style of politics on an international scale-a style of persuasive rather than forceful intervention that remains faithful, as he says is "inevitable and unobjectionable" for a Westerner, to "distinctively Western social democratic aspirations".

For culture, he has argued, should not matter to politics on an international scale any more than it matters on the national scale. "We can suggest that UNESCO think about cultural diversity on a world scale in the way our ancestors in the seventeenth and eighteenth century thought about religious diversity on an Atlantic scale: as something to be simply ignored for purposes of designing political institutions." Rorty does indeed speak in the name of human rights. He does so, at least, on occasions when he can thereby chide the academic left for a selective or nonexistent concern for human rights-the inevitable counterpart, he suggests, of its respect for cultural diversity. He refers for example to what Levi-Strauss once disdainfully called "UNESCO cosmopolitanism," the sort of cosmopolitanism which is content with the status quo, and defends it in the name of cultural diversity.

Such cosmopolitanism was, when UNESCO was founded

in the 1940s, prudently and respectfully silent about Stalinism; nowadays it remains prudently and respectfully silent about religious fundamentalism and about the blood-stained autocrats who still rule much of the world. The most contemptible form of such cosmopolitanism is the sort which explains that "human rights" are all very well for Eurocentric cultures, but that an efficient secret police, with subservient judges, professors and journalists, at its disposal, in addition to prison guards and torturers, is better suited to the needs of other cultures.

The alternative to this sputious and self-deceptive kind of cosmopolitanism is one with a clear image of a specific kind of cosmopolitan future: the image of a plane wide democracy. The ponderous sarcasm in this passage is perhaps a sign, however, that Rorty is not entirely comfortable with his position and there is no secret about why he should experience some discomfort. He has amously and controversially criticized the very universalism that he seems here espouse.

He has argued, specifically, that "humanity" and "planet-wide" justice are vaporous and unproductive abstractions and that people act, and should by appealing instead to local solidarities of a smaller but more concrete so. Of course, Marxists themselves cannot feel totally secure with regard to universal compassion or human rights, which is why Eagleton's sarcasm, too, should perhaps be read as evasive or symptomatic. But Eagleton's counterclaim to the universal does suggest a point namely, that Rorty's case against the cultural left is seriously qualified by his own continuing but unacknowledged commitment to culture, a commitment especially and crucially asserted on the international scale.

The "planet-wide democracy" Rorty says he wants -

and that the elitists of the cultural left are supposedly willing to do without becomes impossible because democracy requires a public, and the domain of the international, as Rorty sees it is the domain of the private: the domain of the cultural. On the international level, Rorty himself seems to acknowledge the existence of nothing but culture. The sort of attention Rorty feels should be paid to cultural diversity on a world scale is spelled out in an essay called "Private Irony and Liberal Hope". To transcend one's given ethnocentrism, he argues, is after all an excellent ambition - so long as the ambition remains private. "Ironists," he writes, "are afraid that they will get stuck in the vocabulary in which they were brought up if they only know the people in their own neighborhood, so they try to get acquainted with strange people (Alcibiades, Julien Sorel), strange families (the Karamazovs, the Casaubons), and strange communities (the Teutonic Knights, the Nuer, the man darins of the Sung)." "Ironists read literary critics, and take them as moral advisors" he goes on, "simply because such critics have an exceptionally large range of acquaintance".

An exceptionally large range of acquaintance may well have a deprovincializing, anti-ethnocentric effect on one's sense of self, and this is all to the good. What is not good, for Rorty, is to believe that such an effect can or should be public, in the double sense that it can have a broad popular appeal, and that it can be transmuted, therefore, into actual political institutions.

The privacy of culture permits us to put ourselves in other people's places without feeling we have to do anything about it. The refusal of ethnocentrism is not strictly speaking an action, so it can never be more than private. To be public is necessarily to be ethnocentric.

"The rise of literary criticism to preeminence," Rorty writes, and with it the rise of ironists, has "widened the gap between intellectuals and the public". That is, the same gap that he accuses the cultural left of culpably enjoying, in the New York Times article, is here described as the inevitable and proper result of the cultural lefts concern with culture, a concern that he himself declares should not be more public, should not be allowed to escape from the domain of the private. For we must uphold "a firm distinction between the private and the public".

Literature and its ironies constitute a sort of synthesis: privacy with and even perhaps for others, but privacy all the same. In other words, despite the "range of acquaintance" metaphor, these others are not necessary or even possible conversational partners. That key meaning of the term "public" does not include them. And therefore they need not be dragged into practical discussions about reality, whether political or otherwise. They constitute, that is, not a new international public sphere, but what can only be called the international private sphere.

It is this logic, rather than his momentary and inconsistent sarcasm at the expense of the cultural left, that expresses itself in Rorty's account of human rights for Amnesty International. Decisively and disturbingly, Rorty also places human rights in the private sphere.

Asked by Amnesty to speak in 1993, in the midst of horrifying reports of Serbian "ethnic cleansing," Rorty did not describe human rights in the public vocabulary of justice or law, which would presumably hold domestically. He described them as a private matter of imagination, of "sympathy," of literature. Progress in human rights will not be made by winning support for universals, by getting more and more people to overcome the parochialism of "kinship and custom by inducing them to accept the universal "obligations imposed by recognition of membership in the same species". It will be made by "manipulating their sentiments". For progress in human rights thus far "seems to owe nothing to increased moral knowledge, and everything to hearing sad and sentimental stories".

Human rights talk, Rorty argues, should aim at inducing "the sort of reaction that the Athenians had more of after seeing Aeschylus' The Persians than before, the sort that white Americans had more of after reading Uncle Tom's Cabin than before. You can and should talk about justice, and then go on to legislate accordingly-the problem with the cultural left, remember, is that it did not. But you can only talk about justice, it appears, within your own nation. Extended across national borders, matters of justice become not legislation but literature. Or (in a phrase Rorty borrows from the Argentinian jurist Eduardo Rabossi), they become "human rights culture".

Now Rorty is right in a sense. As employed by human rights advocates, the expression "human rights culture refers to the goal of creating social conditions in which human rights are more likely to be respected. But the phrase also acknowledges that human rights are a culturally specific product. And, as the advocates also acknowledged if more intermittently, this culture of human rights which can be described from without, as well and as badly as other cultures are described - is a culture whose particularity sometimes interferes with its laudable political aims, for example when it unconsciously assumes its own universality and doesn't pay enough attention to its particular interlocutors. But Rorty's use of the phrase makes a different point. In describing human rights as cultural rather than juridical, and thereby denying them any foundational status, he is not merely taking up the (to my mind, inescapable) challenge of supporting human rights without positing any universal human nature a definition of humanity known in advance on which those rights can be based. What it means not to have a foundation, he implies is indeed to exist on the level of culture, on the level of such and sentimental stores. But this is true only beyond the nation. For there is such a thing as law, and is what politics is properly about. And law has *a* better foundation. But laws visits, for Rorty only within the nation.

One reason is the fact that no supranational executive power exists at present, or is likely to exist in the near future. But if even the prospect of such a world state excites a east as much worry as relief, especially in liberals concerned with individual freedom, then it seems doubtful that its absence is treated as the decisive factor. Rotry identification of the international with the private would seem to rely less on conventional liberal stage (for which the "public" is strictly speaking the state as opposed to the market) than on a strange swerve in this own more original nation of the public with democratic dialogue. Strangely, it *is* only within the nation that Rotry is willing to recognize that other foundation on which law is presently based, the alternative to culture or aesthetics that he calls "conversation" or "solidarity" or "consensus."

Democracy and Redistribution

It is pertinent to note that if those affected by decisions are to have influence over those decisions, they must be consulted. Where there is no public, there is no democracy. It should thus come as no surprise that, talk of "Planet-wide democracy" notwithstanding, Rorty's most recent writing chooses not the democratic and reform-minded

James but the aristocratic and aesthetic Nietzsche as the figure who should preside over international realities."

The idea that democracy should be championed within our borders but might have to be abandoned outside them is precisely the double-standard relativism, you recall, for which Rorty had earlier ridiculed the left and its supposed "UNESCO cosmopolitanism." But this inconsistency is not something to which the left can have a single or simple reaction. Yes, Rorty's willingness to let the line between national and international settle his divided loyalties to democracy and to culture does tend to confirm some of the left's fears about the meaning of a left-liberal alliance. It implies that alliance with liberalism would mean giving up, in the name of a proper effort to reduce domestic inequalities, any effort to correct the even greater inequalities that separate rich nations from poor nations. In this case, of course, joint defense of the social welfare state would become an explicit defense of fortress America, a decision to protect by withdrawal from the world a prosperity gained in large part through exploitation of the world.

That program might be a fantasy- it would not result in any withdrawal from the process by which the world's resources continue to be converted into our commodities and profits -but it could have very real consequences as a stick to beat the left on such issues as immigration and foreign policy. But these fears, however reasonable, should not be the end of the story, for we cannot be content with the real international consequences that our commitment to culture already produces.

When Rorty identifies the cultural and the international in order to lessen the importance of both, he also challenges the cultural left to formulate that connection differently.

And he challenges us, if only indirectly, to formulate it in such a way as to invite the effective participation of liberals. He also suggests, again indirectly, that they are closer to us than they may think. The essay in which Rorty steps away from the goal of expanding democracy to an international scale, entitled "Who Are We? Moral Universalisrn and Economic Triage," is equally interesting for another of its shifts. If Rorty has earlier appealed to democracy as a higher value than culture, here he trumps democracy itself with the still higher value of economic redistribution.

He writes:

> "James took for granted the universalistic assumption, common to Christianity and the Enlightenment, that our moral community should be identical with our biological species ... This amounts to the project of distributing the planet's resources in such a way that no human child lacks the opportunities for individual development, the life chances, available to any other human child."

Now we will move to natural law and human rights.

5

Natural Law and Natural Rights

> "Always remember the soundest way to progress in any organization is to help the man ahead of you to get promoted."
>
> —*L.S. Hamaker*

Here in the present chapter an elaborate discussion of nautral law and human rights is being given.

The natural law tradition, perhaps best articulated in its early stages by the Greeks, recognized that there is something beyond agreed social norms, something deeper than any given contemporary values and something more important than the specific laws decreed by a particular government that should govern the way people relate with one another. The basic approach of natural law philosopher was that by using their intellects all persons could come to know various rules and aspects of the natural law.

The natural law concept was further developed by the Stoics. According to Horowitz:

> "In Stoic thought, man is intimately linked to God through the substance of his soul that he shares with God containing within himself a part of God, man contains within himself the law of

nature, for God is the law of nature. ... At birth man has the faculty to reason, the ability to form common notions, the seeds of knowledge and the spark of divinity. These four possessions are really one - the special gift of God to man. This gift gives man not the full-blown knowledge of natural law, but the potentiality to attain this knowledge. The Stoic synthesis of the doctrine of natural law carries the conviction that natural law is knowable by men who develop their God-given faculties."

(Horowitz, *"The Stoic Synthesis of Natural Law' in the History of Ideas*).

Another writer stressed that the Stoics:

> "introduced a principle that proved to be the turning point in the history of ethical, political, and religious thought. To the Platonic and Aristotelian ideal of justice there was added an entirely new conception: the conception of the fundamental equality of man."
>
> (Cassirer, *The Myths of the State*)

Natural law was re-discovered by philosophers and theologians in Medieval Europe and applied creatively to some of the problems and questions of their day, with Thomas Aquinas among the most articulate advocates of this period. However, the most significant contemporary breakthrough in the natural law tradition took place in Europe, during and at the end of World War II, as a response to the positive laws enacted in Nazi Germany. The International Covenant on Human Rights which is a direct product of this most recent development of natural law is based on the view that there exist basic rights rooted in natural law.

Natural law and basic rights transcend the laws and power of any given state and government. Human beings do not have rights because they are given by and recognized by a government; all persons have rights because these rights are rooted in a natural law. Since these rights are rooted in natural law, no government can deprive any person or any group of human beings of their basic rights.

Natural law has been subjected to attacks from three quarters:

First, there have been those Protestant thinkers who, emphasising the corruption of the human race, have denied the capacity of natural, unredeemed man to respond to moral law. This is manifestly absurd, and in fact has the effect of undermining the Christian faith. For how can Christians come to recognise Jesus to be 'the way, the truth and the life', without some inkling of what is the way, the truth and the life.

Secondly, there are legal positivists who deny the existence of any laws or rights that are not already present in legal form. But a Theistic view of the world will always want to insist that human laws ultimately derive their validity from, and are subject to correction by, a higher moral law. The moral obligation to obey the law is not derived from the law itself, and law is, rightly, in a constant process of flux. Unjust laws, such as the Group Areas Act in South Africa, are not morally binding (though it may be deemed prudent on occasions to adhere to them).

Thirdly, moral philosophers have sometimes doubted whether the concept of natural law has any meaning. Certainly few today would want to defend the thesis that what occurs naturally, that is, in unimpeded nature, is ipso facto, a design carrying moral obligation.

However, what is protected by the concept of natural law is the conviction that human beings are moral beings; that irrespective of any religious beliefs they have the capacity to recognise moral truths; and that whatever differences of culture or religion may divide us it is possible for people of differing backgrounds to engage in moral discourse with one another on the basis of at least some common assumptions. Indeed the development of modern human rights law is a remarkable tribute to natural law in this sense. From the United Nations Charter in 1945 to the latest Instrument of the ILO people of the most diverse backgrounds have agreed on a long series of law and rights. This agreement and the discussion that produced it pre supposes capacity for moral, and not just legal, discourse that belongs to human beings as such: that is natural.

Some, in the natural law tradition, see natural law and natural rights as being closely bound up. Jacques Maritain, for example, after arguing that human beings, as such, have a destiny and that destiny is natural and therefore obligatory for us, wrote:

> "If man is morally bound to the things which are necessary to the fulfilment of his destiny, obviously, then he has the right to fulfil his destiny; and if he has the right to fulfil his destiny he has the right to the things necessary for this purpose".

Remarkably, whatever reservations moral philosophers may have about natural law there appears to be less reluctance to use the phrase natural rights. There are, of course, still those who say, like Bentham, that it is a non-sensical notion and that talk of them as 'natural and inprescriptible' (that is, inalienable) is just 'nonsense upon stilts'. But, from a Christian perspective, they exist; not just as legal rights but as moral rights which undergird and subject to improvement all legal rights.

These rights are natural; that is, they belong to all human beings qua human beings and they can be recognised as such by everyone whatever their religious convictions. Although, as was suggested earlier, Christians were active in the formulation of rights in the American Declaration of Independence, and though the concept of natural law contains an implicit recognition of human rights, there is nevertheless a niggling doubt in some quarters about whether talk about rights is really compatible with Christianity.

First, there is the idea that a creator can do as he likes with his creatures. Creatures, it is said, have no rights: and this, if true, seems to undermine any idea that creatures have rights even between themselves at the creaturely level. But, as we argued earlier, God has created man in his own image: and God himself recognises and respects the supreme worth of what he has created.

Secondly, there is the notion that Christian ethics is an ethic of duty, rather than rights. Even if this is true, duties presuppose rights. My duty not to murder presupposes the right of other human beings to life. But it is not certain that the Christian faith is committed to a duty-based, rather than a goal-based, right-based, or value-based moral philosophy. It is true that the common starting point for Christian action is doing the will of our heavenly Father. But this will is for the well-being and flourishing of his creatures. How we decide what will make for their well-being and flourishing is illuminated by the biblical revelation. But in moral reflection on this, the notions of right, good and value, as well as duty, all have a place. Indeed, if Christianity is committed to the idea of the worth of each individual person (as opposed to any collective goal) it would seem to favour the move being made in some quarters towards a right-based moral philosophy.

Thirdly, there is the idea, derived in particular from the Sermon on the Mount, that Christians should be in the business of waiving their rights rather than asserting them. This raises very complex and disputed questions of how we are to interpret and apply the perfectionist strand in Christian ethics. This element, focused on the Sermon on the Mount, acts as an absolute standard which judges all our human compromises, but that it does not, under the conditions of sinful finite existence, take away our civic duties and rights. We have both duties to the state and rights under it.

Those rights exist whether or not individual Christians choose in certain circumstances to waive particular rights. For, of course, there is the world of difference between choosing to waive one's own rights - the right to sue, for example, as mentioned in Matthew 5:40 - and urging others to waive theirs. Rather, in the world in which we live, a world in which there are so many powerless, Christian love is best shown by championing the rights of the weak, and expanding the areas in which their rights are respected, against the vested interests of the powerful.

Unfolding Rights

We all know, Human rights are rooted in moral values. Because of this legal recognition of rights *is a* dynamic historical process. It is as the result of a gradual - too gradual - process that rights have become enshrined in declarations, conventions and covenants that go to make up International Human Rights Law. First it was the barons who obtained recognition of their legal rights in the Magna Carta of 1215, and not only their own rights but the rights of all freemen. Then came the Charter of 1354 when Edward III introduced the important concept of 'due process of law'.

In the eighteenth century the process was speeded up and the bourgeoisie obtained some of the political and economic liberties that we take for granted in the West today. In our own century we have seen those political and economic rights being claimed by the great mass of human beings. The fact that the legal recognition of rights has been the result of a long, slow historical process need not lead us back into a legal positivism or make us think that the concept of a natural right has no meaning apart from its legal expression. Dworkin draws a distinction between a concept and a conception. For example, the American Constitution lays down the concepts of 'due process of law' and the equal protection of the law for all citizens, but it did not tie future citizens to the particular conceptions of due process and equal protection in force in the late eighteenth century. Yet guided by these fundamental concepts they were to express conceptions of them in varying circumstances.

A natural human right is, in Kantian terminology, the combination of a transcendent ideal with a categorical imperative: a combination about which some philosophers are sceptical but one which Christian theologians, for whom both fact and value are ultimately grounded in the being of God, are sympathetic to. Nor does the idea of truth being revealed by a long historical process embarrass theologians (though some would reject the possibility).

As the doctrinal truths of the Bible were only spelt out

as the result of a process of development so also ethical truths have taken time to be seen in their fullness. In the early Christian Church there was a new equality before God. Rich and poor, bonded and free - all shared the common meal and knew they were equally subject to the just judgment of a loving God.

As Paul wrote:

> "There is neither Jew nor Greek, there is neither bond nor free, there is neither male nor female: for ye are all one in Christ Jesus".

The full implication of that epoch-making text has not even now been fully secured legally, politically, economically, or even ecclesiastically. Yet the history of the West over the last 1,000 years can be seen, in part, as a grasping of its implications. One of the disadvantages of the old natural law concept was that it blinded people to the dynamic, developmental possibilities inherent in ethical insight. The ruling picture, taken from the political structures of the time, is hierarchical, submissive and static. The super-sovereign, God, gives his eternal law. Human beings through the use of their reason reflecting on nature, grasp this as natural law. In addition, God reveals his divine positive law. The two are brought together by secular rulers and the Church to provide laws, both secular and ecclesiastical, for Christendom.

All is revealed, and all is enforced through a hierarchy from God to the lowest magistrate. The human duty is to listen, submit and obey. Some basic rights are, of course preserved in this system.

From time to time prophetic voices, like that of Francisco de Vitoria in the sixteenth century, pointed out ways in which basic rights were being denied. But this magisterial, architectonic system hardly encouraged the drawing out of insights that challenged and called for change in the received wisdom. By contrast, modern theologians who are concerned with human rights associate them closely with Liberation Theology.

As the phrase suggests, the central emphasis of this theology is that God is ceaselessly active in history, liberating human beings from all that enslaves and oppresses them. From the Exodus to the liberation struggles of today God is freeing people, not just from sin and death but from oppressive systems and structures. This involves Christians today in a new commitment to the poor, in line with God's bias to the poor revealed in the Bible. As Jose Bonino has put it: For the vast majority of the population of the world today the basic 'human right' is 'the right to a human life'. The deeper meaning of the violation of formal human rights is the struggle to vindicate these larger masses who claim their right to the means of life ... the drive towards universality in the quests of the American and French revolutions, the aspirations in the UN Declaration, finds its historical focus today for us in the struggle of the poor, the economically and socially oppressed, for their liberation.

Again, Moltmann, who has written a number of essays on human rights, has said:

> "I think that only with this concrete starting point in the theology of liberation can universal theories- and declarations about the freedom of man be protected from their misuse."

Since World War II the main sources for Christian reflection and comment on human matters have been not so much the works of individual theologian as the Vatican in the form of various papal encyclicals and the World

Council of Churches (WCC) through the pronouncements of the Genera Assemblies. They have played their part in forming the general commitment to human rights that has produced the current body of human rights law. The modern human rights movement began immediately after the end of World War II as part of the determination to build a better world, a world in which what had happened in Germany could never happen again. Some of the pressure for human rights has continued to grow from the desire to protect individuals from brutal governments, whether in South America, Africa, or the Middle East.

But the human rights movement, not least in its Christian form, has also been shaped by two other major factors. First, Communism in the Soviet Union. For here is not just one more example of an oppressive government from whom the individual needs to be protected: here is an ideology which offers a particular challenge, both intellectual and practical, to the whole liberal notion of human rights. We may summarise that challenge under three heads:

1. liberal notions appear, from a Marxist standpoint, too individualistic.
2. they are therefore too much concerned with individual freedoms and too little with the basic necessities of life; those necessities which are a basic right for all people and which must be a priority for governments to obtain them.
3. from the liberal standpoint, the USSR has seemed gravely to violate certain fundamental freedoms.

The World Council of Churches, of which the Russian Orthodox Church is a member, has tried to maintain a delicate balance between affirming the fundamental freedoms that are dear to liberals, including Christian liberals, while not jeopardising the precarious position of the Orthodox, who are required to be loyal to policies of their government. The other major factor, besides Soviet Communism, that has shaped the Christian debate on human rights is the concern, particularly by Roman Catholics in South America, for the basic necessities of life at present being denied millions of poor by oligarchies working in conjunction with world capitalism. From this is derived the close connection between human rights and liberation theology that has just been mentioned. From this point of view human rights as a championing of the individual against the power of the state has seemed very much a European concern. What is wanted, on this perspective, is intervention by the state on behalf of the poor against the tyranny of unrestrained capitalism of modern age.

These different contexts and needs highlight the fact that human rights are not a static once-for-all achievement, but rather a moral imperative that requires constant, appraisal and application. Nevertheless, these rather different empress can be held together by Christian theology. First there is the supreme value of each individual, as has already been discussed. But in Christian theology man is a social being. Mind itself is social reality. Man is made in the likeness of God not as a solitary individual but as a person in relationship, reflecting the relationship within the Trinitarian Godhead.

The end of man is the communion of saints - a fellowship of persons knit together by love. This has important implications for human rights. For it means that freebooting individualism is a denial of the essential nature of human personhood. We are persons only in relation to other persons. The other person's welfare is my welfare. It means too that the state, which expresses and builds up man as a social being, has a particular responsibility for the well-being of all its citizens.

The function of the state is not simply to mark out the pitch or mow the grass so that free individuals can compete with one another. The state has a duty to intervene to safeguard the interest of the more vulnerable, for they too are members of the whole and it is the welfare of all people as part of the whole that is at stake. If the Christian emphasis upon the dignity of each individual acts as a check on all views in which a collective goal is regarded as supreme (not least the Communist vision) the Christian emphasis on the social nature of man rules out a merely minimal concept of the state. This is reinforced by Christian insight into the sinfulness of man. For if the presence of sin necessitates checks and balances on the potential tyranny or rulers, it no less leads to the necessity of state intervention against the unrestrained pursuit of gain by the strong, and the need for a protective cloak around the most vulnerable. This debate about the nature of political society is reflected among moral philosophers in the debate between freedom and equality. In the Western liberal tradition the freedom of the individual has long been regarded as the most fundamental of human rights.

H.L.A. Hart has written:

> If there are any moral rights at all it follows that there is at least one natural right, the equal right of all men to be free.

More recently Ronald Dworkin has argued that, on the contrary, the most fundamental of rights 'is a distinct concept of the right to equality, what I call the right to equal concern and respect'. Dworkin argues that this is in fact the deep theory underlying our notions of fairness, including the well-known account of John Rawls. Dworkin does not sit lightly to freedom. On the contrary, he has argued that the just requirement of a system based on equal concern and respect is to take seriously the choices of each individual."

How better to treat them equally than to give them equal choice. Nevertheless, it is equality that is fundamental for Dworkin and his formula of equal concern and respect has distinct theological reverberations. It immediately calls to mind a God who, it is said, values every hair of our head; a God who mixes with the rejected and invites them into his Kingdom of Eternal Life. On his side God promises loving kindness and faithfulness. In return he asks of man - what? To share in his work; to share in the risk of creation. Creation is a risk: some of the time it seems a risk that was not justified. But God invites us to share in his great work, his work for the well-being and flourishing of all his children. In particular he invites us to share his commitment to the most vulnerable, to ensure their rights as human beings.

Yin Yang

Basically, Yin-Yang is not a religion, but a philosophy that has its roots in early Chinese world views. These world views were developed into a philosophy over the centuries with significant new concepts being added by Taoist philosophers and later, from the 11th century onwards, by Neo-Confucianist Philosophers. It gives a succinct description of the relationship between the forces of Yin and Yang and how their inter-action leads to and creates all that exists.

As per to the Yin-Yang theory, the universe came to be as a result of the interactions between the two opposing universal forces of yin and yang. The existence of the universe is seen to reside in the tensions resulting from the universal force of non-being, or yin, and the universal force of being, or yang. Whatever is experienced simultaneously has being and lacks being; it comes into being and passes out of being. But this is just to say that it is being pulled between the forces of yin and yang.

The changing world that is experienced - that is characterized as nature -can exist only when there is both being and non-being, for without being there is no coming-into-being, and without non-being there is no passing-out-of-being. Hence yin, the negative, and yang the positive, are required As a source of nature.

This basic world view was taken one step further by Lao Tzu who posited the existence of the Tao as the source of both Yin and Yang or being and non-being. Prior to Lao Tzu the principles of yin and yang were known. They were regarded as opposites, and all the things in the world were considered to be the production of the interaction between yin and yang. But yin and yang, opposed as light and dark, cold and warm, being and non-being, etc., being opposite, could not of their own nature either produce themselves or interact with each other.

A third something providing a basis and a context for the interaction of yin and yang was required. The great contribution of Lao Tzu was his recognition of Tao as the source of being and non-being - of yin and yang - and the function of Tao as the basis for the interaction of yin and yang.

As the absolutely first principle of existence' Tao is completely without characteristics. It is itself uncharacterized, being the very source of and condition of all characteristics. In this sense it is non-being. But it is not simply nothing for it is the source of everything. It is prior to all the existing things, giving them life and function, constituting the oneness underlying all the diversity and multiplicity of the world.

Lao Tzu himself puts it this way:

> "The Tao that can be told of is not the eternal Tao; the name that can be named is not the eternal name. The Nameless is the origin of Heaven and Earth; the named is the mother of all things."

The importance of Tao lies in the recognition that there is something which is prior and anterior to the various particular things that exist in the world, something which gives unity to all the existing things and which determines the very existence and function of everything. What that something is cannot, of course, be said, for whatever can be talked about is limited and determined, for it is the very condition of limits and determinations. ...

The functioning of the Tao is eternal and recurrent, producing all things and directing their activities. ... The lesson the Taoists drew from nature is that when a thing reaches one extreme, it reverses and returns to the other extreme. Chou Tun-i helped to lay the foundations for Neo-Confucianism in the 11th century.

Describing the production of the yin and yang from the Great Ultimate, Chou Tun-i says:

> 'The Great Ultimate through movement generates yang. When its activity reaches its limit, it becomes tranquil. Through tranquility the Great Ultimate generates yin.'

His explanation of how the yin and the yang are produced from the Great Ultimate leans heavily on the Taoist notion of 'reversal as the movement of Tao.' According to the Taoists, reality *is* the manifestation of the reversing of Tao, as it goes from one extreme back to the other. Thus he goes on to say,

> When tranquility reaches its limit, activity begins. So movement and tranquility alternate and become the root of each other, giving rise to the distinction of yin -and yang, and the two modes are thus established.'

So the new addition by the Neo-Confucianists is the existence of a Great Ultimate that underlies and permeates all that exists.

The Great Ultimate, which produces all things and determines their functions, is a combination of stuff (ch'i) and principle (h). The nature of things is the result of what they are and how they function. The stuff of which they are made is their matter, or ch'i and their function is their principle, or IL When ch'i and li are in harmony, things are in order and there is a grand harmony. Since the Great Ultimate represents a harmony of ch'i and 11, order is the law of the universe.

Before going on, let us look at the symbol that represents Yin Yang. The circle is divided not by a straight line, but by a curved line, representing that there is not a fixed, rigid division between two opposites such as light and dark, past and present, male and female, etc.

This underlying principle supports and nourishes the constantly changing beings in the universe as well as being the basic unifying factor or element that maintains the unity of all that exists.

The harmony between the two opposites results in a balance. This balance or harmony is not fixed but is constantly changing; there is a continuous creative tension between the two sides. According to Yin-Yang thinking, any tendency towards domination by one force will eventually lead to an increase by the opposite side, so as to attain a new balance between the two sides.

Relationship between Historical Schools of Natural Law

The Yin-Yang approach is quite similar. In the Yin-Yang world view, there is an underlying Great Ultimate or Tao which is the source of life and nature, as well as being a unifying force of all that exists; this Great Ultimate is in nature and can be discovered by those who seek it. Some would argue that according to the Yin-Yang philosophy there is never any real progress or development; there is, only a return to the previous balance that existed before one side exerted too much dominance over the other. Yin-Yang approach can be applied in a way that would enable people to refer to and build on previous historical experiences that attained a certain balance. People could address new and unique historical problems by adding their own knowledge and wisdom in a creative way so as to correct new imbalances and attain a new historical balance.

This approach would not seek to return to the balance achieved in some particular "golden age," but would deal with new experiences, circumstances and problems in a way that would aim for the attainment of a new balance based on the new material and scientific conditions present in society, as well *as* the new level of human awareness reflected in current political, social and economic consciousness. By creatively trying to understand and improve oneself and the world, individuals and groups of persons can not only learn to live their lives according to the natural law and the Great Ultimate (and religious values and principles), but can also add to their knowledge of what these are. The Greeks and Stoics and early Taoists were able to articulate certain formulations which clearly articulated their understanding of these laws and principle and values, not unlike the work their contemporaries did in many fields of science. For example, astronomy reached a very high level of understanding that could be attained by use of the naked eye, nightly observations, and mathematical formulations. The basic astronomical principles they developed were the basis of study and further research until the breakthroughs that were attained first by the use of increasingly larger telescopes and in more recent years by the Hubble Space Telescope. Using this creative Yin-Yang approach, each new development in natural law is rooted in and flows from the insights articulated by earlier natural law exponents. These new insights are then added to and become part of the "new balance" of basic principles that later generations can draw on and creatively apply to the new problems of their own society.

Each new step taken by a later generation, in their response to the questions and problems of their day, leads to a deeper understanding of and the further evolution of these basic principles, values and laws; in turn each step in the evolutionary process leads to the attainment of a new harmony. Future generations will then have a richer, better articulated presentation of the natural law to apply to their own new questions, problems, conflicts and social imbalances. In short, the goal of this Yin-Yang "adapted approach" is not to keep these natural law principles, values, laws, etc. in a museum or a "safe place." The goal is to recognize that they are relevant to and can be applied to issues facing people if they are seen not as fixed, absolute and never-changing answers to any problem, but rather are considered as principles, values, laws, etc. that can be adapted for the purpose creative dialogue with contemporary problems.

> "For years statements issued by various meetings of Catholic Bishops always included a reference such as " Asia is the birth place and the cradle of all the world's great religions."

"Religions did great things in the past when they responded to people and the needs of society. But what are they doing today? They confine themselves to rituals and the concerns of the temples, churches and monasteries."

There is thus a dilemma, for if the values of religion are extremely important to our lives, why do so many people consider them not that meaningful in relation to finding ways to deal with the problems of today's world?

Love, justice, peace, honesty, truth, dignity, fairness, etc. are values which flow from and are at the core of all religions. These values would appear to be not only invaluable for human life, but also necessary for the proper functioning of human and social relationships. Why then are religions, which embody in their traditions such important values, not able to respond in meaningful ways to many of the concerns and questions of people today? One thinks that many of the religions are not unlike valuable bronze urns or pots that have been unearthed by archeologists. These bronze wares are deemed too valuable to be used in ordinary homes or restaurants, so they are placed in museums where they can be studied and admired by experts and interested people. The same is true for gold, silver and bronze coins that are discovered at some ancient site or a hole in some farmer's field. The coins will not buy you a bus ticket, but they will be eagerly sought after by coin collectors and museums who will put them away in a safe place to protect them or a well guarded museum cabinet for people to admire.

Religions are all too often satisfied with preserving the customs and practices and prayers and rituals of the past, without asking about their relevance to contemporary problems. All too often religions have answers without first knowing what the question or problem is.

All too often the starting point of religious representatives is their own concerns rather than starting by first listening to and entering into dialogue with people and societies facing new forms of old problems as well as new problems. Religions have basic principles and values that they can and, do offer to believers. A sociologist might note that there are many values and principles shared by all religions.

It is a universal practice to say good-bye to a deceased person, even though the forms, prayers, ceremonies, etc. vary greatly from culture to culture. Since this is such a universal practice, stretching throughout history and across cultures, can we say that it is rooted in some universal natural law. Religions throughout the world are intimately involved in funeral services and celebrations. The right to a decent funeral that flows from a natural law could be categorized as not only a right that is natural to all human beings but can also be listed as a basic human right as well as a basic religious right.

In Sri Lanka, some one decade back, many families were deprived of this basic right to say good-bye. Government troops and officials carried out an official policy of making people "disappear." The result was that relatives were never even sure if their brothers, sisters, fathers, mothers, cousins, uncles, aunts, sons and daughters were dead, as most of the "disappeared' were. Relatives never had a chance to show their last respects and to say a formal, dignified good-bye.

What was the response of religious leaders when this basic human right, also a religious right, was violated? People asked why religious leaders kept silent when a whole group of school children "disappeared?" But these "disappearances" did not only occur in Sri Lanka. Similar scenes were made part of human history by power hungry, insensitive politicians throughout the world. Fortunately we know of some religious persons who spoke up and condemned these disappearances, but all too often religious leaders remained silent or even perhaps added their support for government policies that allowed the disappearances to take place.

Thousands of years before Sri Lankans had to face this horrendous experience of not being able to hold a funeral for loved ones who were considered enemies of the state, a Greek dramatist presented the a similar problem to his audiences. The dilemma faced by the main character was that she had to choose between supporting the decree proclaimed by a new ruler or upholding some more basic - natural - law. In the drama "Antigone" written by Sophocles more than 2.000 years ago, a dead body lay outside the city walls. Creon, the new king had issued an edict that no one was to bury the body; anyone who violated the edict would be stoned to death.

Antigone, a young woman was in a dilemma as she stared at the body - for the corpse was the body of her brother. Antigone was well aware of the universal practice and custom, rooted in some natural law that she considered higher than the edict issued by the king which demanded that a dead person be given a proper burial rather than having his body devoured by dogs.

She was forced to choose between providing a decent burial for her brother and obeying the laws of her uncle, the new king. Again one chooses the funeral because it is so clearly religious. However there are many other basic human values which are also well within the scope of natural law and probably also well within the scope of religious concerns, but which are increasingly claimed by politicians as being in their realm. In the perfect world of the Yin-Yang harmony, there is no clear cut division between religious values and political concerns. The line between the two is curved and there is a little bit of one within the other. There is a constant tension between the two sectors and there should also be a dialogue between them in regard to new questions that are raised by social groups and new developments in society, such as those raised by science and scientists.

An unhealthy relationship occurs when one part of the circle allows itself to be dominated by the other, for then an imbalance and a dis-harmony results. When one part of the circle withdraws from the dialogue and the encounter, the creative tension is removed and there is no healthy development, for only one side dominates: no further progress is made. Progress only results from the healthy, creative dialogue between both sides of the circle, slowly evolving towards a new harmony. Without the tension and dialogue, a healthy harmony cannot be attained.

This approach can be applied to all social tensions: man-woman; humans-natural environment, majority groups-minority groups; etc. The focus here is only on human rights. In the Yin-Yang approach one advocates, the goal of religions is not to take over a state and establish religious-based laws as has been done in some countries. In this Yin-Yang approach, the goal is not for religions to hide away in churches and temples and mosques and leave these issue to politicians to decide.

In this Yin-Yang approach, there is the need for a creative dialogue between politics and religion. Religions must recast and re-kindle their principles and values and enter into dialogue with all sectors of society, including political leaders so as to ensure that they help to create a healthy harmony in society. This Yin-Yang approach would encourage religions to maintain a healthy harmony in their own institutions by ensuring that there is a constant dialogue between their activist and contemplative traditions and experience. Contemplation alone, nor activity in society alone sums up the religious experience; both are needed, the dialogue and tension between the two develops a healthy harmony.

The administrators of the world's great religions have to spend so much time and effort taking care of their sociological institutions and preserving the traditions and memories of their faith, that they don't have enough energy and enthusiasm to dialogue with the world. However, theologians, priests, monks, mullahs and ordinary believers can enter into a Yin-Yang dialogue with the world to see how the beautiful values and time-honored principles and morals of their religious traditions can be polished and re-cast to meet the needs of today and tomorrow.

Human rights, like the natural law, are not something static and absolute; human rights are in the process of being articulated, clarified and developed. A better understanding of human rights can evolve from a Yin-

Yang type dialogue among many groups - including those who are part of a religious tradition and members of religious institutions. Without the creative input from religious traditions, the Yin-Yang dialogical tension will be that much poorer.

V.R. Krishna Iyer, an Indian Supreme Court judge wrote an article stressing how the courts and judges must enter into a dialogue with all parts of society to avoid the law becoming a meaningless and withered appendage.

He used to following quote to illustrate his point:

> "Our judges are not monks or scientists, but participants in the living stream of our national life, steering the law between the dangers of rigidity on the one hand and of formlessness on the other. Our system faces no theoretical dilemma but a single continuous problem: how to apply to ever-changing conditions the never-changing principles of freedom."

(Earl Warren, quoted by Justice V.R. Krishna Iyer in Towards *a* Burgeoning of Indian Jurisprudence of Social Action and Public Interest Litigation).

Religions should have the same attitude towards human rights. Perhaps a first contribution of religions could be for all religions to enter into a Yin-Yang dialogue with one another on various aspects of human rights.

For example could religions attain a common position on the rights of children; the rights of political detainees; the rights of women; the right not to be tortured, the right to food, etc.? Could religions delve into their traditions and contribute to a needed dialogue on the Yin-Yang relationship between Rights and Responsibilities? Religions don't have to give final answers and draw up strict rules by which people should live their lives. However, from a Yin-Yang perspective, religions can play a vital role by encouraging people to enter into dialogue with contemporary society and find ways of persuading people to use the many values of religions to deal with and resolve the problems of society.

Specifically in relation to human rights, religions can help to provide a creative atmosphere to remind, encourage, persuade, and at times demand that basic human values be recognized and respected by all. In relation to the further development of human rights and the implementation of human rights religions are not being given a heavy burden to bear. From a Yin-yang perspective religions are being issued an invitation to enter into a dialogue with all those who want to develop human rights so that we can all cooperate in the process to ensure that all persons will enjoy the protection of basic human rights. Concepts of Dharma or Natural Law, have not only a role to play in the enacting of Laws in the most modern democratic systems but also throw light and guide the interpretation and enforcement of the Laws enacted in order to secure justice to the individuals concerned.

Natural law or Dharma commands humane treatment even to those in prison. Prisons are built with stones of law and so it behoves the court to insist that, in the eye of law prisoners are persons, not animals, and punish the deviant 'guardians' of the prison system where they go berserk and defile the dignity of the human inmate.

Prison houses are part of Indian earth and the Indian Constitution cannot be held at bay by jail officials 'dressed in a little, brief authority', when Part III is invoked by a convict. For when a prisoner is traumatized, the Constitution suffers a shock. And when the court takes cognizance of such violence and violation, it does, like the hound of Heaven but with unhurrying chase, and unperturbed pace, deliberate speed and majestic instancy' follow the official offender and frown down the outlaw adventure. To aggravate the malady, we have the fact that a substantial number of the prisoners are under trial who have to face their cases in court and are presumably innocent until convicted. By being sent to Tihar jail they are, by contamination, made criminals-a custodial perversity which violates the test of reasonableness in Article 19 and of fairness in Article 21. How cruel would it be if one went to a hospital for a check up and by being kept along with contagious cases came home with a new disease.

We sound the cocsin that prison reform is now a Constitutional compulsion and its neglect may lead to drastic court action. The word "nature", the cosmic sense, denotes the life force but in the human sense, it denotes the nature of man. The word "nature" literally means the innate quality or tendency of the things or objects, and the word "Just" means upright, fair to proper.

According to R.G. Chaturvedi, the concept of equality is symptomatic of those platitudinous rights which the fathers of the 'American Independence and those of the French Revolution have acclaimed as the 'inalienable' and 'imprescriptible rights of men, the rights which form the essence of manhood, or the rights which cannot be dissociated from being of man without impairing his dignity. The security of these rights is a natural claim of the man upon his, society, and this claim has an impact on the constitution of a State, because the society is now a politically organised unit called the State. The 'State is an association of human beings which is brought into existence by a morally self-possessed society to serve as its imperial agent for making its sense of justice prevail in the justiciable sphere of the social life, and with that end in view endowed with supreme legal authority on condition of exercising it in strict conformity with the moral standards of the Society. The identification of natural law with Divine will or dictates of God may have, quite understandably, vanished at a time when men see God, if they see one anywhere at all, in the highest qualities inherent in the nature of Man himself.

But the idea of a natural law as a morally inescapable postulate of a just order, recognizing the inalienable and inherent rights of all men and women and equals before the law persists. We can reject Blackstone's theory of natural rights as totally irrelevant for us today.

In celebrated commentaries of Blackstone on the Laws of England, Blackstone said:

> "This law of nature, being coeval with mankind, and dictated by God himself, is of course superior in obligation to any other. It is binding over all the globe in all countries, and at all times: no human laws are of any validity, if contrary to this; and such of them as are valid all their force and all their authority, mediately or immediately, from this original".

Modern jurisprudence conceives of all rights as relative or as products of particular socio-economic orders, yet, the idea that man, as man morally has certain inherent natural primordial inalienable human rights goes back to the very origins of human jurisprudence. It is found in Greek philosophy. If we have advanced today towards what we believe to be a higher civilisation and a more enlightened era, we cannot fall behind what, at any rate, was the meaning given to "personal liberty" long ago by Blackstone.

Now, what are the Fundamental Rights? They are embodied in Part III of the Indian Constitution and they may be classified thus:

(i) right to equality,
(ii) right to freedom,
(iii) right against exploitation,
(iv) right to freedom of religion,
(v) cultural and educational rights,
(vi) right to property, and
(vii) right to constitutional remedies.

They are the rights of the people preserved by our Constitution, 'Fundamental rights' are the modern name for what have been traditionally known as 'natural rights'. As one author puts it 'they are moral rights which every human being everywhere at all times ought to have simply because of the fact that in contradistinction with other beings, he is rational and moral. They are the primordial rights necessary for the development of human personality.

They are the rights which enable a man to chalk out his own life in the manner he likes best. Our Constitution, in addition to the well-known Fundamental Rights, also included the rights of the minorities, 'untouchables' and other backward communities, in such rights. What has said does not mean that Fundamental Rights are not subject to change or modification. In the most inalienable of such rights a distinction must be made between possession of *a* right and its exercise. The first is fixed and the latter controlled by justice and necessity.

Take for example Article 21. 'No person shall be deprived of his life or personal liberty except according to procedure established by law.' Of all the rights, the right to one's life is the most valuable. This article of the Constitution, therefore, makes the right fundamental. But the inalienable right is curtailed by a murderer's conduct as viewed under law.

The deprivation, when it takes place, is not of the right which was immutable but of the continued exercise of the rights. The concept of Fundamental Rights Has been accepted in all modern democratic constitutions. The philosophical foundation of Fundamental Rights according to some is natural law, and the history, of rights of man is bound with the history of natural law. This makes Fundamental Rights, natural rights. Natural rights are supposed to be moral rights which every human being everywhere at all times ought to have simply because of the fact that in contradiction with other beings, be is rational and moral. Natural Law Theory, however has lost some of its appeal to modern jurists. The framers of the Indian constitution did not accept the theory of natural law for the purpose of incorporating Fundamental Rights in the constitution. Hence, it would be incorrect to describe the Fundamental Rights incorporated in our constitution as natural rights or inalienable rights. They are the political and civil rights guaranteed by the Constitution. The Supreme Court in Golaknath case by a majority had laid down that the Fundamental Rights are moral or natural rights. However, this view was abandoned by the Court in Kesavananda Bharti case where the majority held that the Fundamental Rights are not one of the basic structures of the Constitution. Parliament in exercise of its constitutional power deleted during 1978 the right to property from the Chapter of the Fundamental Rights. Both Parliament and the, highest judiciary in India may thereby have abandoned the theory that the Fundamental Rights are the natural right of man.

Natural law had always stressed the duties more than the rights of government and individuals. But during the late 1600s, the natural law tradition began to emphasise natural rights. The change was brought about, largely by the writings of the English philosopher John Locke. Locke argued that governmental authority depends on the people's consent.

According to Locke, people originally lived in a state of nature with no restrictions on their freedom. Then they came to realize that confusion would result if each person enforced his or her own rights. People agreed to live under a common government, but not to surrender their rights of nature to the government instead, they expected the government to protect these rights, especially the rights of life, liberty, and property. Locke's ideas of limited government and natural rights became part of the English Bill of Rights (1689), the French Declaration of the Rights of Man (1789), and the U.S. Bill of Rights (1791). Today, many scholars reject the natural law and natural rights theories. These scholars believe that all laws-including those guaranteeing civil rights-are simply devices that people find convenient, or useful at a particular time. Nevertheless, nearly all civil rights laws have resulted from the theories of natural law and natural rights.

In fact, human rights are universal not only because their roots exist in all cultures and traditions. Their modern universality is founded on their endorsement by all 185 Members of the United Nations. The Declaration itself was the product of debates between a uniquely representative group of scholars, a majority of whom came from the non-Western world. They brought to this historic assignment the recent memories of world war and the ancient teachings of universal peace.

The principles enshrined in the Universal Declaration of Human Rights are deeply rooted in the history of humankind. They can be found in the teachings of all the world's great cultural and religious traditions. Imam Ali, the fourth Khalifa after Prophet Muhammed, instructed the governor of Egypt to rule with mercy and tolerance towards all his subjects:

> "Let the dearest of your treasuries be the treasury of righteous action... Infuse your heart with mercy, love and kindness for your subjects. Be not in the face of them a voracious animal, counting them as easy prey, for they are of two kinds: either they are your brothers in religion or your equals in creation."

Sa'adi, the great thirteenth-century Persian poet, also offered a moving tribute to the values of tolerance and equality among all peoples and nations:

> "The children of Adam are limbs of one another and in their creation come from one substance. When the world gives pain to one member, the other members find no rest. Thou who are indifferent to the sufferings of others do not deserve to be called a man."

Almost 2,000 years ago, Confucius spoke of the dignity of the individual and the tolerance of the State towards the freedom of expression of all its citizens:

> "When the good way prevails in the State, speak boldly and act boldly. When the State has lost the way, act boldly and speak softly."

Now we come to the human rights from religions angle proper.

6

Human Rights from Religious Angle

> "Human nature being what it is, power is always abused. It is to the best interests of society, therefore to see that no individual or group gets too much power or retains it too long."
>
> —*Waldo Lee McAtee*

Since here our concern is to describe human rights from religious angle, every curious reader would like to understand religion in pros and cons. First we will give a vivid account of religion.

What is Religion?

A religion is a system of human thought which usually includes a set of narratives, symbols, beliefs and practices that give meaning to the practitioner's experiences of life through reference to a higher power, deity or deities, or ultimate truth. Religion is commonly identified by the practitioner's prayer, ritual, meditation, music and art, among other things, and is often interwoven with society and politics.

It may focus on specific supernatural, metaphysical, and moral claims about reality (the cosmos and human nature) which may yield a set of religious laws, ethics, and a particular lifestyle. Religion also encompasses ancestral or cultural traditions, writings, history, and mythology, as well as personal faith and religious experience. The term "religion" refers to both the personal practices related to communal faith and to group rituals and communication stemming from shared conviction. "Religion" is sometimes used interchangeably with "faith" or "belief system," but it is more socially defined than personal convictions, and it entails specific behaviors, respectively.

Obviously, the development of religion has taken many forms in various cultures. It considers psychological and social roots, along with origins and historical development.

Religion is often described as a communal system for the coherence of belief focusing on a system of thought, unseen being, person, or object, that is considered to be supernatural, sacred, divine, or of the highest truth. Moral codes, practices, values, institutions, tradition, rituals, and scriptures are often traditionally associated with the core belief, and these may have some overlap with concepts in secular philosophy. Religion is also often described as a "way of life" or a life stance.

The word "religion" as it is used today does not have an obvious pre-colonial translation into non-European languages. Daniel Dubuisson writes that "what the West and the history of religions in its wake have objectified under the name 'religion' is ... something quite unique, which could be appropriate only to itself and its own history." The history of other cultures' interaction with the religious category is therefore their interaction with an idea that first developed in Europe under the influence of Christianity.

A good understanding of the meaning of Christianity before the word "religion" came into common usage can be found in St. Augustine's writing. For Augustine, Christianity was a *disciplina*, a "rule" just like that of the Roman Empire. Christianity was therefore a power structure opposing and superseding human institutions, a literal Kingdom of Heaven. Rather than calling one to self-discipline through symbols, it was itself the discipline taught by one's family, school, church, and city authorities. However at this point the root of the English word "religion", the Latin *religio*, was in use only to mean "reverence for God or the gods, careful pondering of divine things, piety" (which Cicero further derived to mean "diligence"); in other words, there was no sense of a "system" nor even of the Christian power structure but only of spirituality.

Max Müller characterized many other cultures around the world, including Egypt, Persia, and India, as having a similar power structure at this point in history. What we would call religion today, they would only call "law". As Christianity became commonplace, the charismatic authority identified by Augustine, a quality we might today call "religiousness", had a commanding influence at the local level. This system persisted in the Byzantine Empire following the East-West Schism, while Western Europe regulated unpredictable expressions of charisma through the Roman Catholic Church. However, as the Church lost its dominance during the Protestant Reformation and Christianity became closely tied to political structures, religion was recast as the basis of national sovereignty, and religious identity gradually became a less universal sense of spirituality and more divisive, locally defined, and tied to nationality. It was at this point that "religion" was dissociated with universal beliefs and moved closer to dogma in both meaning and practice. However there was not yet the idea of dogma as personal choice, only of established churches.

In the Age of Enlightenment, the idea of Christianity as the purest expression of spirituality was supplanted by the concept of "religion" as a worldwide practice. This caused such ideas as religious freedom, a reexamination of classical philosophy as an alternative to Christian thought, and more radically Deism among intellectuals such as Voltaire. Much like Christianity, the idea of "religious freedom" was exported around the world as a civilizing technique, even to regions like India that had never treated spirituality as a matter of political identity.

In Japan, where Buddhism was still seen as a philosophy of natural law, the concept of "religion" and "religious freedom" as separate from other power structures was unnecessary until Christian missionaries demanded free access to conversion, and when Japanese Christians refused to engage in patriotic events. With the Enlightenment religion lost its attachment to nationality, but rather than being a universal social attitude, it was now a personal feeling, or emotion. Friedrich Schleiermacher in the late 18th century defined religion as *das schlechthinnige Abhängigkeitsgefühl*, commonly translated as "a feeling of absolute dependence". His contemporary Hegel disagreed thoroughly, defining religion as "the Divine Spirit becoming conscious of Himself through the finite spirit." William James is an especially notable 19th century subscriber to the theory of religion as feeling.

Modern Currents in Religion

Sociologists and anthropologists tend to see religion as an abstract set of ideas, values, or experiences developed as part of a cultural matrix. For example, in Lindbeck's *Nature of Doctrine,* religion does not refer to belief in "God" or a transcendent Absolute. Instead, Lindbeck defines religion as, "a kind of cultural and/or linguistic framework or medium that shapes the entirety of life and thought... it is similar to an idiom that makes possible the description of realities, the formulation of beliefs, and the experiencing of inner attitudes, feelings, and sentiments." According to this definition, religion refers to one's primary worldview and how this dictates one's thoughts and actions.

Thus religion is considered by some sources to extend to causes, principles, or activities believed in with zeal or conscientious devotion concerning points or matters of ethics or conscience, and not necessarily including belief in the supernatural. Although evolutionists had previously sought to understand and explain religion in terms of a cultural attribute which might conceivably confer biological advantages to its adherents, Richard Dawkins called for a re-analysis of religion in terms of the evolution of self-replicating ideas apart from any resulting biological advantages they might bestow. He argued that the role of key replicator in cultural evolution belongs not to genes, but to memes replicating thought from person to person by means of imitation. These replicators respond to selective pressures that may or may not affect biological reproduction or survival.

Interfaith Cooperation

Because religion continues to be recognized in Western thought as a universal impulse, many religious practitioners have aimed to band together in interfaith dialogue and cooperation. The first major dialogue was the Parliament of the World's Religions at the 1893 Chicago World's Fair, which remains notable even today both in affirming "universal values" and recognition of the diversity of practices among different cultures. The 20th century has been especially fruitful in use of interfaith dialogue as a means of solving ethnic, political, or even religious conflict, with

Christian-Jewish reconciliation representing a complete reverse in the attitudes of many Christian communities towards Jews.

Secularism and Religion

As religion became a more personal matter, discussions of society found a new focus on political and scientific meaning, and religious attitudes were increasingly seen as irrelevant for the needs of the European world. On the political side, Ludwig Feuerbach recast Christian beliefs in light of humanism, paving the way for Karl Marx's famous characterization of religion as "the opiate of the masses". Meanwhile, in the scientific community, T.H. Huxley in 1869 coined the term "agnostic," a term subsequently adopted by such figures as Robert Ingersoll. Later, Bertrand Russell told the world *Why I Am Not a Christian*.

Atheists have developed a critique of religious systems as well as personal faith. Modern-day critics focus on religion's lack of utility in human society, faulting religion as being irrational. Some assert that dogmatic religions are in effect morally deficient, elevating to moral status ancient, arbitrary, and ill-informed rules—taboos on eating pork, for example, as well as dress codes and sexual practices—possibly designed for reasons of hygiene or even mere politics in a bygone era.

Further, Religious belief usually relates to the existence, nature and worship of a deity or deities and divine involvement in the universe and human life. Alternately, it may also relate to values and practices transmitted by a spiritual leader. Unlike other belief systems, which may be passed on orally, religious belief tends to be codified in literate societies (religion in non-literate societies is still largely passed on orally). In some religions, like the Abrahamic religions, it is held that most of the core beliefs have been divinely revealed.

Religious belief can also involve causes, principles or activities believed in with zeal or conscientious devotion concerning points or matters of ethics or conscience, not necessarily limited to organized religions.

Some Notable Religious Movements

In the 19th and 20th centuries, the academic practice of comparative religion divided religious belief into philosophically-defined categories called "world religions." However, some recent scholarship has argued that not all types of religion are necessarily separated by mutually exclusive philosophies, and furthermore that the utility of ascribing a practice to a certain philosophy, or even calling a given practice religious, rather than cultural, political, or social in nature, is limited. The list of religious movements given here is an attempt to summarize the most important regional and philosophical influences, but it is by no means a complete description of every religious community.

1. Abrahamic religions are practiced throughout the world. They share in common the Jewish patriarch Abraham and the Torah as an initial sacred text, although the degree to which the Torah is incorporated into religious beliefs varies between traditions.

   (a) Judaism accepts only the prophets of the Torah, but also relies on the authority of rabbis. It is practiced by the Jewish people, an ethnic group currently centered in Israel but also scattered throughout the Jewish diaspora. Today, Jews are outnumbered by Christians and Muslims.

(b) Christianity is centered on the life and teachings of Jesus of Nazareth as presented in the Gospels and the writings of the apostle Paul (1st century CE). The Christian faith is essentially faith in Jesus as the Christ, the Son of God, and as Savior and Lord. As the religion of Western Europe during the time of colonization, Christianity has been propagated throughout the world. However, Christianity is not practiced as a single orthodoxy but as a mixture of Catholicism, Eastern Orthodoxy, Oriental Orthodoxy, and many forms of Protestantism. In the United States, for example, African-Americans and Korean-Americans usually attend separate churches from Americans of European descent. Many European countries as well as Argentina have established a specific church as the state religion, but this is not the case in the United States nor in many other majority Christian areas.

(c) Islam refers to the religion taught by the Islamic prophet Muhammad, a major political and religious figure of the 7th century CE. Islam is the dominant religion of northern Africa, the Middle East, and South Asia. As with Christianity, there is no single orthodoxy in Islam but a multitude of traditions which are generally categorized as Sunni and Shia, although there are other minor groups as well. Wahhabi Islam is the established religion of the Kingdom of Saudi Arabia. There are also several Islamic republics, including Iran which is run by a Shia Supreme Leader.

(d) The Bahá'í Faith was founded in the 19th century in Iran and since then has spread worldwide. It teaches unity of all religious philosophies and accepts all of the prophets of Judaism, Christianity, and Islam as well as additional prophets including its founder Bahá'u'lláh.

(e) Smaller Abrahamic groups that are not heterodox versions of the four major groupings include Mandaeism, Samaritanism, the Druze, and the Rastafari movement.

2. Indian religions are practiced or were founded in the Indian subcontinent. Concepts most of them share in common include karma, caste, reincarnation, mantras, yantras, and darœana. Islam in India has also been influenced by Indian religious practices.

(a) Hinduism is a synechdoche describing the similar Indian religious philosophies of Vaishnavism, Shaivism, and related groups, and is the predominant religion of the Indian subcontinent Hinduism is not a monolithic religion in the Romannic sense but a religious category containing dozens of separate philosophies amalgamated as Sanâtana Dharma.

(b) Buddhism was founded by Siddhattha Gotama in the 6th century BCE. Buddhists generally agree that Gotama aimed to help sentient beings end their suffering by understanding the true nature of phenomena, thereby escaping the cycle of suffering and rebirth (saCsâra), that is, achieving Nirvana. The main schools of Buddhism are Theravada, Mahayana, and Vajrayana.

(c) Sikhism is a monotheistic religion founded on the teachings of Guru Nanak and ten successive Sikh Gurus in 15th century Punjab. Sikhs are found mostly in India.

(d) Jainism, taught primarily by Parsva (9th century BCE) and Mahavira (6th century BCE), is an ancient Indian religion that prescribes a path of non-violence for all forms of living beings in this world. Jains are found mostly in India.

(e) There are dozens of new Indian religions and Hindu reform movements, such as Ayyavazhi and Swaminarayan Faith.

3. Yazdânism is a non-Abrahamic monotheistic category including the traditional beliefs of the Yazidi, Alevi, and Ahl-e Haqq.

4. Religious movements centered in the United States are often derived from Christian tradition. They include the Latter Day Saint movement, Christian evangelicalism, and Unitarian Universalism among hundreds of smaller groups.

5. Folk religion is a term applied loosely and vaguely to disorganized local practices. It is also called paganism, shamanism, animism, ancestor worship, and totemism, although not all of these elements are necessarily present in local belief systems. The category of "folk religion" can generally include anything that is not part of an organization. The modern neopagan movement draws on folk religion for inspiration.

(a) African traditional religion is a category including any type of religion practiced in Africa before the arrival of Islam and Christianity, such as Yoruba religion or San religion. There are many varieties of religions developed by Africans in the Americas derived from African beliefs, including Santería, Candomblé, Umbanda, Vodou, and Oyotunji.

(b) Folk religions of the Americas include Aztec religion, Inca religion, Maya religion, and modern Catholic beliefs such as the Virgin of Guadalupe. Native American religion is practiced across the continent of North America.

(c) Australian Aboriginal culture contains a mythology and sacred practices characteristic of folk religion.

(d) Chinese folk religion, practiced by Chinese people around the world, is a primarily social practice including popular elements of Confucianism and Taoism, with some remnants of Mahayana Buddhism. Most Chinese do not identify as religious due to the strong Maoist influence on the country in recent history, but adherence to religious ceremonies remains common. New religious movements include Falun Gong and I-Kuan Tao.

(e) Traditional Korean religion was a syncretic mixture of Mahayana Buddhism and Korean shamanism. Unlike Japanese Shinto, Korean shamanism was never codified and Buddhism was never made a social necessity. In some areas these traditions remain prevalent, but

Korean-influenced Christianity is far more influential in society and politics.

(f) Traditional Japanese religion is a mixture of Mahayana Buddhism and ancient indigenous practices which were codified as Shinto in the 19th century. Japanese people retain nominal attachment to both Buddhism and Shinto through social ceremonies, but irreligion is common.

6. A variety of new religious movements still practiced today have been founded in many other countries besides the United States and Japan, including Cao Dai in Vietnam.

   (a) Shinshûkyô is a general category for a wide variety of religious movements founded in Japan since the 19th century. These movements share almost nothing in common except the place of their founding. The largest religious movements centered in Japan include Soka Gakkai, Tenrikyo, and Seicho-No-Ie among hundreds of smaller groups.

While superstitions and magical thinking refer to nonscientific causal reasoning, applied to specific things or actions, a religion is a more complex system about general or ultimate things, involving morality, history and community. Because religions may include and exploit certain superstitions or make use of magical thinking, while mixing them with broader considerations, the division between superstition and religious faith is hard to specify and subjective. Religious believers have often seen other religions as superstition. Likewise, some atheists, agnostics, deists, and skeptics regard religious belief as superstition. Religious practices are most likely to be labeled "superstitious" by outsiders when they include belief in extraordinary events (miracles), an afterlife, supernatural interventions, apparitions or the efficacy of prayer, charms, incantations, the meaningfulness of omens, and prognostications.

Greek and Roman pagans, who modeled their relations with the gods on political and social terms scorned the man who constantly trembled with fear at the thought of the gods, as a slave feared a cruel and capricious master. Such fear of the gods (*deisidaimonia*) was what the Romans meant by *superstitio* (Veyne 1987, p 211). Early Christianity was outlawed as a *superstitio Iudaica*, a "Jewish superstition", by Domitian in the 80s AD, and by AD 425, Theodosius II outlawed pagan traditions as superstitious.

The Roman Catholic Church considers superstition to be sinful in the sense that it denotes a lack of trust in the divine providence of God and, as such, is a violation of the first of the Ten Commandments. The Catechism of the Catholic Church states superstition "in some sense represents a perverse excess of religion" (para. #2110).

Superstition is a deviation of religious feeling and of the practices this feeling imposes. It can even affect the worship we offer the true God, e.g., when one attributes an importance in some way magical to certain practices otherwise lawful or necessary. To attribute the efficacy of prayers or of sacramental signs to their mere external performance, apart from the interior dispositions that they demand is to fall into superstition. Cf. Matthew 23:16-22 (para. #2111)

Religion and Philosophy

Being both forms of belief system, religion and philosophy meet in several areas - notably in the study of metaphysics and cosmology. In particular, a distinct set of religious beliefs will often entail a specific metaphysics and cosmology. That is, a religion will generally have answers to metaphysical and cosmological questions about the nature of being, of the universe, humanity, and the divine.

Cosmology

Humans have many different methods which attempt to answer fundamental questions about the nature of the universe and our place in it (cosmology). Religion is only one of the methods for trying to answer one or more of these questions. Other methods include philosophy, metaphysics, astrology, esotericism, mysticism, and forms of shamanism, such as the sacred consumption of ayahuasca among Peruvian Amazonia's Urarina.

The Urarina have an elaborate animistic cosmological system, which informs their mythology, religious orientation and daily existence. In many cases, the distinction between these means are not clear. For example, Buddhism and Taoism have been regarded as schools of philosophies as well as religions. Given the generalized discontents with modernity, consumerism, over-consumption, violence and anomie, many people in the so-called *industrial* or *post-industrial West* rely on a number of distinctive religious worldviews. This in turn has given rise to increased religious pluralism, as well as to what are commonly known in the academic literature as new religious movements, which are gaining ground across the globe.

Religion and Science

Religious knowledge, according to religious practitioners, may be gained from religious leaders, sacred texts (scriptures), and/or personal revelation. Some religions view such knowledge as unlimited in scope and suitable to answer any question; others see religious knowledge as playing a more restricted role, often as a complement to knowledge gained through physical observation. Some religious people maintain that religious knowledge obtained in this way is absolute and infallible (religious cosmology). The scientific method gains knowledge by testing hypotheses to develop theories through elucidation of facts or evaluation by experiments and thus only answers cosmological questions about the physical universe. It develops theories of the world which best fit physically observed evidence.

All scientific knowledge is subject to later refinement in the face of additional evidence. Scientific theories that have an overwhelming preponderance of favorable evidence are often treated as facts (such as the theories of gravity or evolution). Many scientists have held strong religious beliefs (see List of Christian thinkers in science) and have worked to harmonize science and religion. Isaac Newton, for example, believed that gravity caused the planets to revolve about the Sun, and credited God with the design. In the concluding General Scholium to the Philosophiae Naturalis Principia Mathematica, he wrote: "This most beautiful System of the Sun, Planets and Comets, could only proceed from the counsel and dominion of an intelligent and powerful being."

Nevertheless, conflict has repeatedly arisen between religious organizations and individuals who propagated scientific theories that were deemed unacceptable by the organizations. The Roman Catholic Church, for example, has in the past reserved to itself the right to decide which scientific theories were acceptable and which were unacceptable. In the 17th century, Galileo was tried and forced to recant the heliocentric theory based on the church's stance that the Greek Hellenistic system of astronomy was the correct one. Today, however, only 7% of the members of the National Academy of Sciences believe in a god.

Epistemology

Many theories exist as to why religions sometimes seem to conflict with scientific knowledge. In the case of Christianity, a relevant factor may be that it was among Christians that science in the modern sense was developed. Unlike other religious groups, as early as the 17th century the Christian churches had to deal directly with this new way to investigate nature and seek truth. The perceived conflict between science and Christianity may also be partially explained by a literal interpretation of the Bible adhered to by many Christians, both currently and historically.

The Catholic Church has always held with Augustine of Hippo who explicitly opposed a literal interpretation of the Bible whenever the Bible conflicted with Science. The literal way to read the sacred texts became especially prevalent after the rise of the Protestant reformation, with its emphasis on the Bible as the only authoritative source concerning the ultimate reality. This view is often shunned by both religious leaders (who regard literally believing it as petty and look for greater meaning instead) and scientists who regard it as an impossibility. Some Christians have disagreed or are still disagreeing with scientists in areas such as the validity of Keplerian astronomy, the theory of evolution, the method of creation of the universe and the Earth, and the origins of life. On the other hand, scholars such as Stanley Jaki have suggested that Christianity and its particular worldview was a crucial factor for the emergence of modern science.

In fact, most of today's historians are moving away

from the view of the relationship between Christianity and science as one of "conflict" — a perspective commonly called the conflict thesis. Gary Ferngren in his historical volume about Science & Religion states: While some historians had always regarded the [conflict] thesis as oversimplifying and distorting a complex relationship, in the late twentieth century it underwent a more systematic reevaluation. The result is the growing recognition among historians of science that the relationship of religion and science has been much more positive than is sometimes thought.

Although popular images of controversy continue to exemplify the supposed hostility of Christianity to new scientific theories, studies have shown that Christianity has often nurtured and encouraged scientific endeavour, while at other times the two have co-existed without either tension or attempts at harmonization. If Galileo and the Scopes trial come to mind as examples of conflict, they were the exceptions rather than the rule.

Eastern Religions

In the Bahá'í Faith, the harmony of science and religion is a central tenet. The principle states that that truth is one, and therefore true science and true religion must be in harmony, thus rejecting the view that science and religion are in conflict. 'Abdu'l-Bahá, the son of the founder of the religion, asserted that science and religion cannot be opposed because they are aspects of the same truth; he also affirmed that reasoning powers are required to understand the truths of religion and that religious teachings which are at variance with science should not be accepted; he explained that religion has to be reasonable since God endowed humankind with reason so that they can discover truth. Shoghi Effendi, the Guardian of the Bahá'í Faith, described science and religion as "the two most potent forces in human life."

Proponents of Hinduism claim that Hinduism is not afraid of scientific explorations, nor of the technological progress of mankind. According to them, there is a comprehensive scope and opportunity for Hinduism to mold itself according to the demands and aspirations of the modern world; it has the ability to align itself with both science and spiritualism. This religion uses some modern examples to explain its ancient theories and reinforce its own beliefs. For example, some Hindu thinkers have used the terminology of quantum physics to explain some basic concepts of Hinduism such as Maya or the illusory and impermanent nature of our existence.

The philosophical approach known as pragmatism, as propounded by the American philosopher and psychologist William James, has been used to reconcile scientific with religious knowledge. Pragmatism, simplistically, holds that the truth of a set of beliefs can be indicated by its usefulness in helping people cope with a particular context of life. Thus, the fact that scientific beliefs are useful in predicting observations in the physical world can indicate a certain truth for scientific theories; the fact that religious beliefs can be useful in helping people cope with difficult emotions or moral decisions can indicate a certain truth for those beliefs.

Mysticism focuses on methods other than logic, but (in the case of esoteric mysticism) not necessarily excluding it, for gaining enlightenment. Rather, meditative and contemplative practices such as Vipassanâ and yoga, physical disciplines such as stringent fasting and whirling (in the case of the Sufi dervishes), or the use of psychoactive drugs such as LSD, lead to altered states of consciousness that logic can never hope to grasp. However, regarding the latter topic, mysticism prevalent in the 'great' religions (monotheisms, henotheisms, which are perhaps relatively recent, and which the word 'mysticism' is more recent than,) includes systems of discipline that forbid drugs that can damage the body, including the nervous system.

Mysticism (to initiate) is the pursuit of communion with, or conscious awareness of ultimate reality, the divine, spiritual truth, or Deity through direct, personal experience (intuition or insight) rather than rational thought. Mystics speak of the existence of realities behind external perception or intellectual apprehension that are central to being and directly accessible through personal experience. They say that such experience is a genuine and important source of knowledge.

Esotericism is often spiritual (thus religious) but can be non-religious/-spiritual, and it uses intellectual understanding and reasoning, intuition and inspiration (higher noetic and spiritual reasoning,) but not necessarily faith (except often as a virtue,) and it is philosophical in its emphasis on techniques of psycho-spiritual transformation (esoteric cosmology). Esotericism refers to "hidden" knowledge available only to the advanced, privileged, or initiated, as opposed to exoteric knowledge, which is public. All religions are probably somewhat exoteric, but most ones of ancient civilizations such as Yoga of India, and the mystery religions of ancient Egypt, Israel (Kabbalah,) and Greece are examples of ones that are also esoteric.

Members of an organized religion may not see any significant difference between religion and spirituality. Or they may see a distinction between the mundane, earthly aspects of their religion and its spiritual dimension. Some individuals draw a strong distinction between religion and spirituality. They may see spirituality as a belief in ideas of religious significance (such as God, the Soul, or Heaven), but not feel bound to the bureaucratic structure and creeds of a particular organized religion. They choose the term *spirituality* rather than religion to describe their form of belief, perhaps reflecting a disillusionment with organized religion, and a movement towards a more "modern" — more tolerant, and more intuitive form of religion. These individuals may reject organized religion because of historical acts by religious organizations, such as Christian Crusades and Islamic Jihad, the marginalisation and persecution of various minorities or the Spanish Inquisition. The basic precept of the ancient spiritual tradition of India, the Vedas, is the *inner reality* of existence, which is essentially a spiritual approach to being.

Basically, the word `myth' has several meanings.

1. A traditional story of ostensibly historical events that serves to unfold part of the world view of a people or explain a practice, belief, or natural phenomenon;
2. A person or thing having only an imaginary or unverifiable existence; or
3. A metaphor for the spiritual potentiality in the human being.

Ancient polytheistic religions, such as those of Greece, Rome, and Scandinavia, are usually categorized under the heading of mythology. Religions of pre-industrial peoples, or cultures in development, are similarly called "myths" in the anthropology of religion. The term "myth" can be used pejoratively by both religious and non-religious people. By defining another person's religious stories and beliefs as mythology, one implies that they are less real or true than one's own religious stories and beliefs. Joseph Campbell remarked, "Mythology is often thought of as *other people's* religions, and religion can be defined as mis-interpreted mythology."

UNDERSTANDING RELIGIOUS CONFLICT

Differences in doctrine and ritual may at times create a certain social distance between religious communities. They may, on occasions, impede social interaction. But they do not in themselves - and this must be emphasised over and over again - cause conflict.

On the contrary, for the most part of Asian history, the different religious doctrines, practices and symbols have co-existed without too much antagonism or enimity. What this implies is that religious conflict is often conflict between religionists, not religions. Some followers of a particular religion may, for a variety of reasons, clash with some followers of another religion. For most religious conflicts reveal that invariably there are individuals and groups on both sides of the divide who do not approve of the hatred and bitterness generated by the contending forces. They try to reach out to one another and to make peace.

This happened in the midst of the riots following the partition of India and Pakistan in 1947 or assassination of Mrs. Indira Gandhi in 1984. It should also be noted that not all who participate in religious riots are religious, in the conventional sense of the term. Studies have shown that many rioters who shout religious slogans are often totally ignorant of their religious teachings. In practice some of them may even be leading lives which are at variance with the moral precepts of the religions they profess. Though there has been conflict in the name of religion, we must be willing to recognise that, on the whole, different religious communities have lived side by side in various parts of Asia, without having to confront one another. Some of them have not known any serious religious conflagration.

If we take a longer view of history, the absence rather than the presence of conflict has characterised relations between Hindus and Muslims in India. Buddhists and Hindus in Sri Lanka and Buddhists and Muslims in Thailand. History also tells us that religious conflict in precolonial Asia appears to have been less frequent and perhaps even less intense. There was, of course, religious prejudice between different communities. Writing about Hindu-Muslim relations in the early part of the 11th century, the well known Muslim scholar, Al-Beruni, for instance, notes that the Hindus looked upon the invaders as outcastes and "recoiled from the touch of the impure barbarian Muslims". Inspire of this early aversion - an aversion to invaders who had caused great ruination rather than to an alien people with an alien faith -Hindu attitudes towards Muslims and vice-versa, improved over the next one or two centuries. By the time of the reign of the great Mughal emperor Akbar (1556-1605), there was significant fusion of Muslim and Hindu cultures. Compared to the pre-colonial period, ties between Hindus and Muslims in general in contemporary India seem to be less harmonious. This is also true to a greater or lesser degree, of other religious communities in certain other parts of Asia.

Various political and economic developments which have brought about all sorts of changes to the human environment are largely responsible for this deterioration in inter-religiousties. It is these developments which we shall now examine.

Electoral politics and elite manipulation of mass sentiments have had an adverse impact upon religious communities in countries like India, Sri Lanka and Malaysia, With the advent of competitive party politics in these multi-religious societies, party leaders try to mobilise support and maximize their popularity by exploiting the fears and hopes of this or that religious community,

It is not just the religious sentiments of the majority community which ruling elites manipulate. From time to time, they also manipulate the religious feelings of minorities in their societies. It has been pointed out, for instance, that Mrs. Gandhi like Rajiv and perhaps even V.P. Singh sometimes found it efficacious to pander to the Muslim gallery because this assured them of the community's block vote. The manner in which Rajiv Gandhi capitulated to pressure from orthodox, conservative Muslim groups on the Shah Bano controversy has often been cited as a case in point. Block Muslim electoral endorsement, as long as the support of the Hindu majority is also assured, is a boon to any political party in India.

Elite manipulation of majority and minority religious sentiments for electoral purposes is not the only reason why religious tensions build up and sometimes lead to religious conflicts. The modern nation-state itself may also be a factor, The nation-state has a personality of its own in the international arena. Because it has a personality, it often seeks to promote an identity which is unique and distinctive. To do this, the nation-state clothes itself in the cultural or religious garb of the majority community. The culture or religion of the majority therefore becomes the accepted identity of the nation, both internally and externally.

As the state begins to promote this identity through specific policies and programmes, the minority cultures and religions feel threatened. The ensuing atmosphere of insecurity sometimes results in religious tension and conflict. What makes it worse is when the nation-state which has identified itself with the culture or the religion of the majority community also develops authoritarian tendencies. An authoritarian state by its very character would seek to exercise maximum political control Since the mechanics of control and dominance would be in the hands of elites from the majority community minority cultural or religious groups would feel alienated and estranged from the political process. They would not be able to participate meaningfully in national politics even if limited avenues are made available to them.

However, it can be argued that this has been happening in Sri Lanka, especially after 1981' when political authoritarianism grew stronger and stronger with the centralization of power in the hands of the President. A similar pattern is beginning to unfold in Malaysian politics. So far we have looked at some of the political factors which are responsible for the deterioration in inter-religious ties. Some of these political factors have also contributed, directly or indirectly, to the growth of certain cultural attitudes within multireligious societies in Asia which are inimical to religious harmony.

Because the Malaysian state is so closely identified with the Malay-Muslim majority, sections of the community have begun to feel that the other religions have no role to play in the nation's public life. While Islam which is the nation's official religion is given ample coverage over radio and television, the minority religions are totally excluded from the air-waves. Minority religions are also not taught in Malaysian schools. Islam, on the other hand, is a compulsory subject of study for Muslim children from primary to upper secondary school level. Very few Muslim feel that it is wrong to treat the minority religions in this manner, especially when their adherents constitute almost 44 per cent of the total population. The inability to see this as an injustice of sorts - though the Malaysian Constitution does provide for the practice of various faiths - is a consequence of the type of mental conditioning that takes place within a populace when its religion enjoys symbolic and substantive state power. Religious minorities too sometimes develop certain cultural attitudes which are antithetical to a genuine relationship with the majority community.

In India, it is true that sections of both the Muslim and Sikh minorities have sometimes displayed exclusivist tendencies. They are reluctant to seek common ground with Hindus so that certain shared values and principles of living would evolve over time. The demand by some Muslims for a separate, independent state in Kashmir, like the call by some Sikhs for Khalistan, have emerged, in part, from this desire for an exclusive homeland. Such pleas fail to take into account the magnitude of the challenge facing a polity like India which must maintain a degree of unity while celebrating its rich religious and cultural diversity. More than cultural attitudes, it is the interplay of economic forces which has aggravated the relations between different religious communities in certain parts of Asia.

We have already alluded to one of the major economic

causes of religious strife; the propensity of ruling elites to manipulate religious sentiments when they fail to deliver the goods. Indeed, diverting the attention of the masses from their economic and social woes by igniting the religious emotions of the people is a favourite tactic of ruling elites in a number of countries. It is a tactic which has worked over and over again.

But there are other factors too. When an economy is not growing fast enough to provide jobs to the rapidly expanding army of unemployed people, it is quite likely that some of them would fall prey to the mechanations of communal agitators. Riots in India and Sri Lanka in the last decade or so, show that it is always easy to arouse the religious passions of angry, frustrated youths who dare not even hope for gainful employment. This is why economic stagnation or an economy which is growing very slowly is often a bane to good relations between different religious communities. Likewise, if a religious community which has been living side by side with another community, suddenly experiences rapid economic progress and outdistances its neighbour, there is bound to be some resentment which could give rise to tensions and even riots. Sometimes the economic dislocation of a certain segment of a particular community could result in religious tensions especially if those who had benefited from this dislocation happen to be members of another religious community. Uneven development - that is development which benefits certain strata within a region while leaving other groups in other regions lagging behind - can also generate tensions if one region is more heavily populated by a certain religious group and another region has a preponderance of another religious community.

To divide the local population, the British popularised

the idea that the Mughals had desecrated Hindu places of worship in Ayodhya. By propagating this view, they simultaneously sought to project themselves as "sympathisers" of the Hindu majority, while the Mughals - the immediate predecessors of the British - were made out to be oppressors of the Hindus and enemies of Hindu culture and tradition. Just as the colonial impact upon contemporary religious conflicts in Asia merits attention, so too the manipulations of imperialist powers. Given the resurgence in different religious traditions, imperialist powers like the United States can be expected to monitor carefully trends and tendencies within these movements to see how they will impact upon its interests : It is an open secret that some years now - and especially after the Islamic revolution in Iran in 1979 - the United States has been deeply concerned about the rise of radical, revolutionary Islam.

Notably, mainstream American and Western media are determined to denigrate Islam, in particular that brand of Islam which insists on its own autonomy and refuses to acquiesce with American political and military dominance of the globe. One should not be surprised if as a result of its desire to control revolutionary Islam, particularly in West Asia, which incidentally is the world's leading exporter of petroleum, the United States foments conflicts between Muslims and other religious groups. As long as suspicion, hatred, and animosity exist between Muslims and non-Muslims in certain key areas of the world, it would be a little less difficult for the United States to perpetuate its dominance.

It is obvious from our analysis that no one factor can explain why religious conflict occurs. A variety of factors - political, cultural, economic, historical and contemporaneous

- impinge upon religious conflicts in Asia. Let us now find out how we can check this kind of conflict. There will have to be comprehensive political reforms aimed at reducing the potential for religious conflict. The human rights of each and every citizen should not only be acknowledged but also observed in practice. Every citizen, whatever his or her religious affiliation, should enjoy the freedom of expression. Every citizen, whatever his or her religious affiliation, should have the opportunity to participate in public life, Every citizen regardless of her creed, should feel that she can contribute effectively to the political development of her nation. Every citizen, irrespective of the faith he professes, should have the right to aspire for any political office in the land. It is not just individual's rights and liberties that should be guaranteed. In multi-religious societies where each and every community is conscious of its identity, community rights should also be protected. Each and every community should be secure in the knowledge that neither the state nor anyone else poses a threat to its religion or its language and culture. Every community should have the right, within the bounds of the nation's constitution, to develop its religion for the well-being of its adherents. Individual and community rights are one thing. What is equally important is the political structure.

We have seen that multi-religious societies where power is concentrated in the hands of the executive tend to develop authoritarian characterstics and are sometimes insensitive to the just pleas of their minorities. Even those multi-religious societies in Asia which are formally structured as federations, seem to centralize power with their national capitals. In all these countries, there is an urgent need for effective devolution of power and authority. If regions, provinces and states are given more powers to administer their own affairs, it is quite conceivable that the religious and cultural communities associated with particular provinces or states, will feel that they have greater control over their own destinies.

It will also be possible to give due ,consideration to the special economic and cultural needs of certain communities. Devolution of power and authority is an acknowledgement that religious and cultural communities deserve autonomy and freedom within the framework of a larger, loosely-structured polity. Such a polity will not - as it is often feared by advocates of strong government - encourage centrifugal tendencies.

It will not strengthen separatist demands. On the contrary, it is quite likely that when communities enjoy genuine autonomy and freedom, they will be less inclined to break from a Centre which may be perceived as accommodative in attitude and democratic in character. Indeed, autonomy will be meaningful only if some of the other institutions of a democratic society are strengthened and enhanced. Parliament, for instance, should play its role as an effective instrument for legislation.

It should function as the body deliberating national policies and not surrender its authority to, some presidential clique or party caucus. The judiciary should protect its independence and integrity, whatever the costs and consequences. The police, the armed forces and other law-enforcing agencies should, at all times, retain their impartiality and objectivity. The media should establish its credentials as a fearless advocate of truth and justice.

It should never pander to religious bigotry of cultural chauvinism. Political parties, trade unions and social action groups should champion what is right and oppose what is wrong without succumbing to the pulls and pressures of communalism. It is important to emphasise all these duties and responsibilities for a simple reason. A great deal of havoc has been caused by institutions which are expected to protect the public good but instead degenerate into strongholds for perpetuating communal dissension and strife. The police and armed forces, in particular, in a number of multi-religious societies have developed an unsavoury reputation for being biased against particular groups and for brutality. So bias is the situation that one sometimes wonders whether the behaviour of security personnel in certain communal conflagrations is not one of the main causes for the unbroken cycles of violence. This is why any political reform which seeks to minimise the potential for religious conflict should have on its agenda, the creation of disciplined security personnel, capable of self-restraint and of Impartial administration of justice.

As important as political reform is economic reform. To curb the propensity among the unemployed to swell the ranks of rioters in communal disturbances, it is crucial that rapid, sustainable economic growth is encouraged. For economic growth which has as its main thrust the creation of jobs for the young in particular will reduce the level of social frustration.

Youth, as a whole, will become less susceptible to religious chauvinism. In fact, if the economy is growing rapidly, if it is easy to find jobs and if those who are employed enjoy social mobility, people will become much more secure and contended. The ensuing economic stability will inevitably generate the conditions for a healthier political atmosphere. Malaysia is a good example of a multi-religious society which, comparatively speaking, has known much more Interethnic harmony than many other countries, mainly because of its impressive economic development. For more than three decades now, it has registered consistently high growth rates which have helped to keep unemployment down, while expanding economic opportunities for all ethnic communities.

In fact, it is this reality of a growing 'economic cake' which has enabled the government to give special assistance to segments of the indigenous Malay-Muslim community, without causing too much unhappiness amongst the non-Malays and non-Muslims. An active and dynamic private sector provides sufficient scope for the absorption and expansion of non-Malay, non-Muslim capital and enterpreneurial skills. Multi-religious societies in Asia whose economies are not expanding fast enough should devise more imaginative and creative strategies to promote growth and development, Private initiative and enterprise expressed through market relations is a vital pre-requisite for rapid, sustainable growth. But it must be a market which is at the same time responsive to ethical values and conscious of its social responsibilities. Apart from encouraging private enterprise, attempts should also be made to increase productivity through massive investments in education and training. Effective human resource development has played a key role in increasing economic productivity in Malaysia and other successful newly industrializing countries like South Korea, Taiwan and Singapore.

Definitely, it is a pity that there are multi-religious societies in Asia burdened with colossal communal problems which have spent much more of their scarce financial resources on their armed forces and military hardware than on education and training. If these countries had their economic priorities right at the time of Independence there might have been less religious strife today. By emphasising growth and enterprise, we do not mean to downplay the importance of equitable distribution of wealth and opportunities in the endeavour to reduce religious conflict. Our analysis of the causes of religious conflict has shown quite clearly that absolute poverty and economic disparities which sometimes assume an ethnic dimension, are serious threats to social harmony. Absolute poverty especially when it affects substantial segments of certain communities should be eradicated through a variety of measures ranging from agrarian reform and the establishment of small-scale industries to education and infra-structure development. In many multi-religious societies, the government lacks the will to eliminate absolute poverty.

Sometimes this is because of the influence upon government of certain vested interests which benefit directly from the perpetuation of poverty. If governments in countries like India and Sri Lanka had the will, they would also try to reduce economic disparities particularly when they have implications for inter-ethnic ties. Much more attention would be given to the education and training of disadvantaged groups to enable them to catch up with the others. More employment opportunities would be created for disadvantaged groups by facilitating economic activities in hitherto neglected areas.

At the same time, uncontrolled development which dislocates sections of whole communities would not be allowed. Instead, there would be a more planned approach to development which would seek to offset the negative consequences of economic change by re-locating communities in new growth centres or providing alternative employment opportunities to the victims of economic dislocation. Through growth with equity, by integrating enterprise with justice, it should he possible to ameliorate some of the economic conditions which often give rise to religious conflict. But are these economic reforms coupled with the political changes we have discussed, enough to check religious strife. If there is economic prosperity and social justice, on the one hand, and active political participation and viable democratic institutions, on the other, will it be possible for us to control communal passions from running riot? Why is it that in countries where these conditions, are present - the Western democracies for instance - communal feelings are still strong? Is there something else that explains why narrow, bigoted, sectarian notions of religion continue to have such an impact upon so many people?

As far as Asia is concerned, perhaps the problem lies with the way religion is understood and practised. It must be stressed at this point that the problem is not with religion per se. It is not the philosophy or the doctrines; it is not the practices or the rituals which is the issue. To repeat, it is Our interpretation of religion which constitutes the problem. It is the meaning we attach to certain doctrines and rituals which creates difficulties. Over the centuries, most of the followers of most of the faiths in Asia have developed an exclusive view of their particular religious tradition.

God is seen as the God of their particular group, Truth and justice, love and compassion tire perceived as values which are exclusive to their religion. The unity that they seek is invariably the unity of their own kind, Their religion - they are passionately convinced - is superior to other religions. In order to project the exclusive greatness of their religion, they emphasise the forms and practices, the rituals and symbols which distinguish their particular religious tradition from other traditions. They regard these rituals and symbols as ends in themselves.

It is the meticulous application of the rituals of their faith which is their main obsession. The devotion to rituals becomes the ultimate measure of the piety and goodness of an individual. Because most of us are socialized from our infancy into this view of religion, it is deeply embedded in our psyche. Besides, each of us who belongs to a particular religion identifies with a whole tradition which in turn becomes part and parcel of our socialization as we move from childhood to adulthood.

Some of the most significant events in our lives and in the lives of those who are dear to us, are linked to rituals and symbols derived from religion. Religion conditions our values, shapes our thoughts each of us to our religion, It explains, to a large degree, the almost instinctive reaction to the slightest insult or injury done to one's religion. It explains why thousands and thousands of human beings can sometimes work themselves into a frenzy over a religious cause. To affect changes to the way we are socialized into our religion, we have to first, deepen and broaden our understanding of religion. Almost every religion - from the great spiritual experiences of the Australian Aborigines and the American Indians to Sikhism and the Bahai faith - is universal in the message it seeks to convey to humankind. The ultimate reality, the Supreme Being, the God - call it what you will - which religions visualize belongs to all the universes, the whole of humanity. The values of truth and love of justice and compassion are eternal, universal values. The real unity which most of the scriptures envisage is undoubtedly the unity of the whole of mankind, indeed the unity of the whole of existence Itself.

Rites and rituals, forms and symbols are ways of helping us understand this ultimate unity - a unity which is rooted in faith in God and love for all God's creatures. Some of the illustrious mystics in the various religious traditions understood this well which is why they remained truly universal in outlook and attitude and refused to be sectarian. They saw the differences in rituals and modes of worship among the various religions as man-made distinctions.

As one of them observed, "The lamps are different, but the light is the same". We shall now show how this spirit of universal unity exists within a particular religious tradition. Since the tradition we are most familiar with is Islam, we shall draw our arguments from that tradition, though it must be emphasised that most of the other religions have an equally strong commitment to a unity transcending the boundaries of class, community and creed. That the primary purpose of Islam is to achieve the unity of humankind is clearly enunciated in the Quran itself. The Quran declares for instance, "Mankind were one community" and "Lo! this your religion is one religion and I am your Lord, so keep your duty unto me". The reference to 'one religion' is that one universal divine truth revealed to humankind from the very beginning. The Quran says that this was the truth that was revealed to Abraham and to Noah and to Moses and to Jesus. In fact, it makes it very clear that every community on earth has received this universal truth. In the words of the Quran, "There is not a nation but a warner hath passed among them". And what is this universal truth? It is belief in God and doing good. This is lucidly explained in a Quranic verse, "And they say, "None entereth Paradise unless he be a Jew or a Christian. These are their own desires, Say: Bring your proof (of what ye state) if ye are truthful. Nay, but whatsoever surrendereth his purpose to God while doing good, his reward is with his Lord; and there shall no fear come upon them neither shall they grieve".

It is significant that the Quran reiterates over and over again that believing in God and doing good constitute the essence of righteous conduct. This is what all the prophets and seers urged humankind to do. This was the guidance they offered in their noble desire to unite humankind. And yet, the Quran notes with regret, humankind destroyed this universal truth and became sects. It chides humankind for having "broken their religion among them into sects, each sect rejoicing in its tenets". This is an unambigous chastisement of sectarianism.

In the light of what is happening in present-day India, it is worth recalling Kabir's eloquent criticism of false religious differences. He asks, "If God lives in the Mosque, who then lives in the rest of the world? All the Hindus think that Ram lives in the Tirth and in his images; but they have not found Ram. Those who think that Iswara is in the East and Allah is in the West are in profound error. If they want to find Him, they must seek Him in their hearts. They will find Him there." Rejection of religious exclusivism, of sectarian attitudes, and a sincere commitment to the divine truth and to universal unity, as we have hinted a while ago, are by no means the monopoly of any one religion. It should be mentioned in passing that within Hinduism remarkable sages from Shamkara and Ramanuja to Ramakrishna Paramhamsa and Mahatma Gandhi radiated this universal spirit. They too believed that faith in God and love of humankind alone could unite the followers of different religions, As the well-known philosopher S. Radhakrishnan once put it.

> "All outer names are man-made distinctions whereas the reality is faith in God and love of

> man. It is not necessary to do away with differences which distinguish and divide men. We must try to understand them. We must admit faith in the one God of all mankind who is worshipped in many ways."

It is of course true that the universal sentiments of these Hindu and Muslim sages have always remained a subordinate trend within their religions. But this does not mean that we should not try to strengthen this trend by bringing to the fore the sublime values and lofty ideals associated with the universalist's in all the religious traditions.

This is one of the biggest challenges facing all of us who are committed to the quest for harmony and unity among the different communities, in the midst of religious antagonism and conflict. Apart from strengthening the universal trend within our own religion, we should also try to develop a more profound understanding of other faiths. Most of us, even within the intelligentsia, know so little about one another's religion, though we live in multi-religious societies where religion is a living reality. It is only when we acquire knowledge about 'the other's faith' that we will become less attached to the 'us' versus 'them' dichotomy which pervades societies like ours.

This dichotomy, needless to say is one of the most formidable psychological barriers to inter-faith harmony. By trying to understand other religions we will be establishing the basis for genuine inter-faith dialogue. In multi-religious societies, torn asunder by religious strife, there are perhaps few other tasks which are more urgent than this. It is a measure of the depth of our moral bankruptcy and intellectual apathy that we have done so little to promote inter-faith dialogue. Since it is unlikely that governments in our countries will get excited about such dialogues, it is up to us, human rights activists, peace campaigners, environmentalists, feminists and so on, to organize these dialogues on a massive scale. Inter-faith dialogues should be held at all level and in all sectors of society, Unlike the political and economic reforms which we had suggested earlier on, this is something which is within our means. Inter-faith dialogues, properly organized, would help a great deal to-transform a conflict-ridden atmosphere to a harmony laden one.

Inter-faith dialogues, it needs to be stressed, should not just be concerned with metaphysical issues. They should deal with contemporary challenges and some of the perennial social concerns of humankind. If human rights activists, for instance, held an inter-faith dialogue they could examine the question of freedom of expression or of torture from the different religious perspectives. Peace campaigners could dialogue on how religions regard war, violence and the use of force in international relations.

Environmentalists, on the other hand, could analyse how religions view environmental degradation and what sort of ideas they embody on the management of natural resources. It is quite conceivable that through such dialogues the followers of different religions will realize that their doctrines share common perspectives on many of the crucial challenges confronting humanity. For it is true that on the environment, on natural resources, on the function and purpose of government, on the role of leadership, on the family, on community solidarity, on the rights and responsibilities of the human being, and on the values which should be at the core of an ethical society,

Buddhism, Christianity, Confucianism, Hinduism, Judaism, Islam, Taoism and the other religions hold identical positions.

These positions, in a sense, constitute the shared spiritual and moral heritage of humankind. In this shared heritage lies our hope of overcoming the religious conflicts which have pitted community against community in our continent. It is the sacred responsibility of our generation to develop the ideas, values and principles embodied in this heritage so that a new spiritual worldview emerges which will provide an alternative to the dominant secular, materialistic worldview of our age.

This secular, materialistic worldview which has always been uneasy about religion is conflict. It is equally incapable of resolving some of the other colossal problems of our times related to environmental degradation, excessive consumerism, technological mystification, dehumanising life-styles and spiritual alienation. In a sense, this worldview has never really been able to overcome even the more fundamental challenges of economic exploitation and political repression. This is why there is a crying need for an alternative worldview which will incorporate both the perennial wisdom contained in our religious traditions and the wealth of knowledge about political and economic relationships and structures generated by the restless quest of the human mind in the last two centuries. Our alternative universal spiritual worldview will therefore embrace not only values such as freedom, equality and justice but also virtues such as love, compassion, moderation and restraint.

It will not only espouse human rights but also emphasise human responsibilities -including our responsibility to environment, to community, to family and to self. Our universal spiritual worldview will be concerned not only with political and economic structures but will also address issues of morality and ethics. 'It will seek not only the transformation of the social order but also the transformation of the individual self. It is a worldview that will not only celebrate the joy of life but also reflect on the sorrow of death it will be a worldview which will not only protect the particular identities of individual communities but also pursue the universal unity of the whole of humankind. Most of all, it will be a worldview which will not only respect religious diversity but also revere the majesty of a truly universal God,

When that universal spiritual worldview triumphs in the dawn of tomorrow, we, who are witnesses to today's tragedy of religious conflicts, will finally understand what the illustrious mystic Jallaluddin Rumi meant when lie said, "The lovers of God have no religion but God alone."

The Societal Awakening and Resistance

"The next best thing to actually being free, is to be in the struggle for freedom". Such were the words of Lean Alejandro, student activist and youthful leader of the "parliaments of the streets" which resisted against the Marcos dictatorship and later continued to protest against the repressive and elitist policies of the Aquino regime. Having survived the martial law years, Lean Alejandro was brutally assassinated just shortly after he tested the democracy promised by Cory Aquino by rallying his small fishing town around a new type of "People politics" and by running for a seat in Congress. Lean Alejandro was only 27 years old when he was killed. He spoke for a whole generation of "martial law babies" who grew up without any experience of democracy, who were educated under a system which systematically denied human rights, but who went through political awakening and eventually struggled against the social evils in their time.

What, is it that inspired, motivated, and sustained such youthful commitment, dedication, and courage in their resistance against the status quo, even amidst the coldest climate of fear and terror? It is perhaps the realization that under conditions of captivity or political repression, the only real taste of freedom is in struggle and resistance. A more well- known example of courage against formidable odds is Nobel Peace Prize laureate, Aung San Suu Kyi, human rights activist and leader of the democratic movement in Burma, who once said that fear is a habit that corrupts and that can be overcome. She wrote,

> "Within a system which denies the existence of basic human rights fear tends to be the order of the day ... It is not easy for a people conditioned by fear, under the iron rule of the principle that might is right, to free themselves from the enervating miasma of fear. Yet even under the most crushing state machinery courage rises up again and again, for fear is not the natural state of civilized man."

Tyranny and the abuse of power will continue to prevail only if allowed to persist and if communities of people, whether influenced, inspired, or motivated by religious beliefs or other ideals, are not able to resist and struggle for change. Sadly, most religions have condoned, turned a blind eye to, if not participated in the oppression of people. In Asia, *authoritarian regimes* enjoyed the support and sanction, at one time or another, of religious hierarchies. Often, religion has been subject to manipulation by political forces to pursue vested elitist interests, and religious institutions have been perceived by oppressed people as defenders and protectors of the status quo.

This is one reason why human rights abuses and the most brutal violations of human dignity have occurred unnoticed in many societies and go on unabated without eliciting any public outcry. That is only one side of the reality of religion, however. The other side is that, throughout Asian history, there are also many examples of individuals and religious leaders who have shown that religious belief can inspire, challenge, and motivate people to speak out against injustice, to resist tyranny, to act or social change, and to search for new visions of more equitable, more just, and more humane societies.

Sr. Mariani Dimaranan, one of the pioneers of human rights work in the Philippines, recalls one incident during the martial law years when she met a woman who was tortured and raped while imprisoned and who had witnessed similar treatment to her colleagues by military forces. Upon seeing Sr. Mariani, this mother of two, frail and slight of build, turned to her in anguish and asked, "Sister, do you really believe that there is a God? If there's really a God of justice, how can he allow this to happen?" What horrors and unspeakable acts against humanity could drive ordinary human beings to deny the existence of God? In the face of massive exploitation and oppression of people, many people have been driven to dig deep into the recesses of their faith and system of beliefs and have been challenged with respect to the idea of "confession" and repentance for the sin of apathy. This has lead towards the undergoing of a personal transformation or "conversion," and eventually, towards making a deep and lasting commitment to human rights and the struggle for social change. Edicio De La Terre, drawing from the dilemmas and experiences of many religious in the Philippines, once wrote about the process of self-transformation, calling it "the passion, death, and resurrection of the middle-class (petty bourgeois) Christian." He said that Christians need to identify with Christ and Christ's suffering and crucifixion, and undergo their own "passion and death" in order to be resurrected into new beings.

John Kelsay and Stunner B. Twiss in the book "Religion and Human Rights" write that it is hard to deny that religious teachings have been a significant factor in the consciousness and life of some of the people most active in pursuing the goals identified with human rights. They cite the examples of such people as U Thant, Muhammad Zafrullah Khan, Dalai Lama, and many others, to remind us that religion has been an important force in fostering concern for human rights. How can religion be a positive force in promoting human rights and inspiring resistance against human rights abuses?

While historically various social forces have used religious symbols and religious resources to justify acts of human rights violations and outright oppression of people, human rights advocates among the religious have asserted the need to re-claim or rediscover religion and the resources within religion that are liberating and that uphold and promote human dignity. Religions continue to attract adherents, especially from ordinary masses of people, only so long as they fulfill and address certain social, psychological, and spiritual needs.

Many seek in religion not its "negative aspects but those positive resources which offer comfort, compassion, a new way of life and thinking, hope for the future, and even perhaps the promise of justice and a new human community. It is these aspects of religion that can be harnessed towards inspiring the courage to resist and struggle against the most evil forms of denial of human dignity.

In most religious communities, however, religious leaders often enjoy the mantle of comfort, isolated from the ordinary flock. Often, they are awakened to act and resist against injustice only when they are able to identify with the victims of human rights abuses or when they themselves have directly experienced suffering. In the Philippines, there was a popular saying during the martial law years that there is no better teacher about state repression than the blow of a policeman's truncheon.

The widespread political awakening of many priests and nuns happened in that critical instant when they themselves tasted the bitter sting of a tear-gas explosion at a peaceful street rally, or were jolted by the sudden burst and crackle of an armalite in the stillness of a morning mass. To sustain courage and commitment in the resistance against injustice, religious communities need to be in constant touch and humble solidarity with the victims of injustice themselves. Ultimately, it is those who have suffered the most injustice who have the resources within themselves in order to overcome fear and who have the inner resolve and wisdom to find a solution and an end to their suffering.

The most difficult and trying challenge for religious believers, however, lies in re-examining, analyzing, and eventually resisting against the notions and practices of their own religion which are unjust, which justify oppression or which deny humanity to others.

Religion and Rights of Women

Remarkably, is no longer something new for the women's

movement within different religious institutions to get their voices heard even though the effect of this movement appears extremely slow compared to its dynamic vitality in non-religious fields. There are organized meetings which have engaged women from different religious backgrounds to discuss oppressive and liberating aspects of their own religions and have tried to interpret scriptures from a women's perspective and take actions against unequal systems etc. The intention is not to take up the struggle of women but to share the reflections on more essential religious motivations of the women's movement. We have talked a lot about equality and a change of concepts of women but what happened was that in the process of realization women themselves became trapped in "the patriarchal system" which they so often criticized. Our motivation was liberation according to the gospel and to search for an alternative society but in reality when women came into the established society segregation among women also started.

Dr. Gabriele Dietrich takes up this problem within feminist theology in her article "On doing theology in South Asia." (Vision, February 95, T.M.A.M. Orientation Center)

> "We have to be careful that we do not just get caught up in the cosmetic changes of giving women more representation and visibility in a basically male denned structure. We may not gain much fighting for women's ordination as long as the whole relationship between ordained of the church and the laity remains as it is."

May be a more serious happening is that when women in developed countries entered the established society, segregation between them and the women in the developing countries (which make up two thirds of women in the world) started to widen and women's issues became segmented.

Holistic Humanism

Despite the Vedas, the Bible, the Koran, the Buddha and Mahavira and that supreme miracle and revolutionary apostle of ahimsa, Mahatma Gandhi, we have forfeited the right to be heirs of a culture of Karuna, Samata and Dharma vis a vis the older inhabitants of Planet Earth. Daily we trample underfoot the first article of the Universal Declaration of the Rights of Animals:

> "All animals are born with an equal claim on life and the same rights to existence".

Is it not a fact that ours is the most cruel and criminal century capable of mighty atrocity not merely in the World Wars it has waged and the Vietnam outrage, Pol Pot barbarity and the Beirut butchery but in the perfection the science of vivisection and the art of terrible exploitation of the weaker species? Are we human and humane or, as Dr. Schweitzer rightly stressed, lacking in fellow-feeling, when he said:

> Our civilization lacks humane feeling. We are humans who are insufficiently humane! We must realize that and seek to find a new spirit. We have lost sight of this ideal because we are solely occupied with thoughts of men instead of remembering that our goodness and compassion should extend to all creatures. Religion and philosophy have not insisted as much as they should on the fact that our kindness should include all living creatures.
>
> In a philosophic work on the relation of moral

> ethics and civilization written before the First World War, I dared affirm that true goodness requires us to respect the lives of all creatures and I was fortunate in having this idea of reverence for life approved by men of all nations and of seeing an immediate start in its teaching to children in schools.

Humanism cannot be halved by denying it to pre-human brethren and compassion is beyond division by refusing it to the Darwinian species. All life is too divinely integral to admit of unnatural dichotomy as man and animal in the wholeness of ecology. No revolution holds out human hope if it is not rooted in heart-deep compassion and is complete in its vision of Creation. The failure of our generation is not that scientific advance is not great enough but that spiritual advance is on reverse gear. If religion means reverence for life - and it does -our civilization must become more religious. If science includes the science of the soul and must possess social sensitivity to higher values, our World Order is currently more philistinic than scientific.

If deeds, not words, are the measure of mercy, we humans of the 20th century have no credentials of culture, judging by the torture we organize in the name of science and religion. What boots it if we observe Wild Life Week with glitter and human 'wild life' spills more blood and brings more tears week after week? The hour for honesty has arrived and the duty to write into Life the poetry of love has come.

'God is Present before you in the form of all living beings. Where are You seeking God, forsaking all these? One who loves all creatures serves God, indeed'.

On Gandhi Jayanti day let us translate quotations

from books and ,reeds from religions into daily life, national policies and community consciousness. Let us actualise the fundamental duty set out in Article 51 (A) of the Constitution:

> 'To protect and improve the natural environment. . . Wild life, and to have compassion for living creatures. . . .'

'The conservation of wild life has acquired urgency for it is relevant for human survival. Such are the linkage between various species in nature that the elimination of any one species creates problems in others sooner or later. Humankind has already destroyed many species. Let us not do more harm. India has always seen life as one. We should set an "ample in conserving Wildlife. Our children should know more about indigenous flora and fauna so that they can feel the oneness and wholeness of life and contribute to a better future for all living creatures'.

Forests and wild life are interdependent. Forests are not trees and plant life alone. Wild life is also the wealth of the country. Wild life lives in the context of nature. Their increase is also subject to the laws of nature. Some persons in their craze for money and sport, upset this process by killing wild animals. This will result in the ecological balance being upset. We should therefore realise that our efforts towards conservation of wild life are basically for our own good. Them aft laws to prevent destruction of forests and wild life. The co-operation of the people is necessary to enforce these laws.

We have got a variety of animals, birds and plant life not found in any other country. We must protect what is still left of our flora and fauna.

Catchwords like 'Beauty without Cruelty' and 'Wild

Life is our national heritage endowed upon us as a trust' are also plentiful. We have Societies for Prevention of Cruelty to Animals and legislations to prevent cruelty to and protect animals. We have voluntary bodies like Blue-Cross Societies and Kindness Clubs. We have animal shelters and pinjarapoles. We have great men from the Buddha down to Gandhi protesting against cruelty to living beings, but all these in totality are but symbolic. We have St. Francis of Assissi pleading for mercy; so too St. George, a martyr for the cause. We have the Koran with a message of kindness to animals:

> 'There is not an animal on the earth,
> nor a flying creature on two wings,
> but they are people like unto you'.

So also the Buddha:

> 'No living thing is to be killed,
> not even any small animal or insect,
> for all life is sacred'.

The Bible too contains a testament of faith creatures :

> 'The righteous man regardeth the life of his beast'.
>
> — *Old Testament*

But humane feeling, in its finer spirit, is a rare ray among the crowd of religious fanatics in practice.

The raw realities of life have a horrid tale to tell. Poaching of wild animals with the connivance of the Forest officials is not uncommon because forest legislation at the enforcement level is not only dead but is a notorious source of corruption. Look at the kedda operations which involve pleasure-seeking, torture and yet the pious men who perpetrate are worshippers of Ganesa! I have seen a bunch of South Indian Women pressing the Indian Embassy in Mexico to get them tickets to witness macabre bull fights where the groaning animal, already speared, bleeds in agony and is killed by the cowardly matador to the delight of sadistic brutes. Look at the circus animals whose suffering is immense and intense and too terrible to bear for those who have sensitised hearts. Whole volumes can be written about circus torture of wild life and yet, neither the Wild Life Board nor the Animal Welfare Board has been able to arouse the consciousness of the community or any political party to arrest this Satanic entertainment. According to Lord Somers :

> . . . Not everything is known of the methods used in training, since it is all done behind a heavy barrier of secrecy. But what has come to the surface is so revoltingly horrible that anyone with any sense of compassion for defencelss creatures must feel that he cannot rest until circuses are banned, at any rate in civilised countries. And the actual training is not the end of the story.
>
> A circus animal spends its life in a cage just large enough to contain it, where it cannot move, and where many animals die. It is kept on a low diet, as a hungry animal is likely to be more amenable. What a life for a naturally active, vital creature which should live in open places! I can assure my readers that I am not exaggerating the situation.
>
> Intense suffering, both physical and mental, is the lot of the circus animal; and the sooner we can break through the barrier of secrecy and reveal the true picture, the better. No Government

would tolerate such a thing if it was possible to prove the facts, but to do this is not easy.

The way stray dogs are caught and dragged, asphixiated and poisoned with all the piteous howls and pathetic struggles, is a negation of humanism. Our local bodies are corporations and, therefore do not have a heart to weep or soul to be damned! Even temple elephants in holy place like Kancheepuram and Chidambaram have their portion of suffering from illness with no one to care.

The height of inhumanity is contained in the Socialist State of Kerala where a recent advertisement was made inviting tenders for certain terrible operations on Wild Life.

Justice is a right even for the beast, if society is civilized enough. Is not homo sapiens a speciesist (like racist) in the sense that he wages chemical warfare through asphyxiation and enzyme inhibition and a host of other torture tactics? Man, in his evolutionary process, has relied heavily on the pre-human species. Today, he is exploiting and extinguishing those older species, so innocent and invaluable.

Man kills or cruelly treats other animals mostly for exploitative ends. He kills elephants for tusks, rhinos for horns, snakes for skins, crocodiles for hides, deer for aphrodisiacs and many other creatures for varieties of versatile pleasures. We torture frogs, rabbits, mice, pigs, primates and other lovely living things for food, cosmetics, perfumes, soaps, toiletries and several other purposes. We pollute air and water and kill birds and beasts and fishes. Research can find alternatives if compassion is a value and corrupt profit is not.

What we need is a mass movement for a new solidarity, a fresh campaign for cosmic karuna, a lively patriotism for preservation of Planet Earth and all that belongs to it all this, ignited by a profound love of beauty of Nature in its wondrous variegation and viability, and kindled by a spiritually unified vision of Creation and its integrity in the eco-system, in short by a dynamic understanding of the divinity in everything.

Issues of Human Rights in Islam

The concept of universal human rights embodies values which not only conflict with other strongly held values and conceptions but which are incompatible with, and subversive of, certain forms of society and social institutions. A.J. Milne has seen the paradoxical implications of this in the United Nation's Universal Declaration of Human Rights which "professes to be a statement of human rights, irrespective of the particular social and political order under which they happen to live," but which "goes on to enumerate a detailed list of rights which presupposes the values and institutions of a certain kind of social and political order, namely liberal, democratic, industrial society."

Having said this, we must also face the paradoxical fact that there is a case for requiring some form of constitutional structure for the nations. They should be subject to the rule of law and with legal safeguards against the various forms of discrimination against, and violation of the rights of their citizens. This is the fundamental problem we face today and a search for some direction for its resolution is always worthwhile. Such a search however should not mean a compromise or an acceptance of hegemony by any one.

It must be recognized that universal claims made in

the name of all are often, in practice, claims on behalf of existing deprived groups or people against the more fortunate. It is also therefore at the same time a demand to surrender the privileges which are enjoyed by some at the cost of other members of society. Claims to universal rights must therefore be seen as claims which can establish universal entitlement, rather than claims which simply have universal support.

> Universal rights necessarily preclude any discrimination or exclusion, whether on grounds of "race, color, sex, language, religion, political or other opinion, national or social origin, property, birth or other status." Maurice Cranston is thus correct when he writes of a human right being something of which "no one can be deprived without a grave affront to justice. There are certain deeds which should never be done, certain freedoms which should never be invaded, some things which are supremely sacred."

While the universal claims on human rights are claims by the deprived, we have to face squarely, the paradoxical fact that the Human Rights Declaration was a product of the concern of the victorious parties after the Second World War. And that the further work on various human rights covenants are also largely the product of the powerful states. Therefore the difficulty we face is who is to monitor human rights and does such monitoring require a violation of the jurisdiction and authority of a state and its territorial integrity. We also need to ask about how human rights impact upon cultural and ideological diversity.

This difficulty is exacerbated by the fact that all such actions which are done in the name of universal and global principles have been at the expense of the Third World and have ended up extending further the hegemony of the North. Dworkin's distinction between weak and strong moral rights; where the latter are those rights which it would be wrong for a government to override simply on the ground that the exercise of the right is not in the public interest, or is contrary to the majority we can be helpful on a theoretical level but still leaves us short of some form of global implementing mechanism. These problems are compounded when we consider the topic "human rights and religion" and increase tenfold when the religion in question is Islam.

Jacques Waardenburg in his article "Human Rights, Human Dignity and Islam" makes some interesting observations about the religious reactions to human rights declarations. He argues that "It is significant that religious leaders nearly always adopted a critical attitude (toward these declarations] to start with. Following that, there were several possibilities of accepting human rights in principle, once it had become clear -that public opinion was increasingly in favour of them." He then goes on to fist these possibilities:

1. That these declarations had nothing new to offer "and that the religions concerned had a concept of human dignity and law which went further or was more profound than the Human Rights Declaration;" and,
2. "To accept human rights as an ethical norm or code, and then to proceed by developing a theological basis for them with an appeal to scripture, particularly by attributing their origin and that of human dignity less to human nature than to God's grace."

He concludes by saying “that most religious responses to the Universal Declaration of Human Rights still reflect an ideological use of these human rights for the sake of the religions concerned, be it apologetically, or polemically. Ideological or not, human rights undoubtedly have a spiritual meaning for religions people just as they have a political meaning in social life.”' This spiritual dimension cannot be ignored and in this paper I want to try and move beyond both apologetic and polemic approaches which religion normally adopts towards the issue of human rights. In order to deal with the comprehensive concepts involved in the theme of human rights and religion it necessary to give a brief definition of belief which grounds these issues and provides the context for a discussion of human rights. For it is clear that the concept of religion is somewhat problematic in this context.

It is characteristic of belief, both that it is the subject of debate, questioning and interpretation by believers and non-believers, that there are different views as to what constitutes a belief, and that among believers themselves there are varying degrees of commitment to the practical implementation of the principles of a given belief. To have a belief in this sense is to have faith. Faith may be seen and understood in terms of the outcome of two quite different kinds of experiences. The first is faith through birth in a society or a community where all, or virtually all, of the members have a particular tradition of belief or set of beliefs.

In contrast is faith through personal conviction which is a matter of the individual struggling, possibly against parental, social and other pressures, to arrive for herself/ himself at the truth. These two faith experiences can lead to situations of tension and conflict as the move to the second type of faith can well be seen as a betrayal of the first kind of faith-indeed as a betrayal of religion itself and of the integrating structures of society. This tension lies at the heart of the issue of religion and human rights and therefore deal with the specific issue of the universal right of freedom of conscience and freedom of religion within the religious sources and specifically Islam as compared to those enshrined in the various declarations and documents dealing with human rights in the international context.

Similarly, Max Stackhouse has indicated that Islam is a religious tradition ill suited to democratic conceptions of society. It simply does not present the individual with those opportunities for freedom of action and association that are characteristic of western Christianity (in certain cases).

Even an otherwise sound scholar such as James Piscatori who can conclude that the respect for life and property which Islam teaches and its practice of tolerance and fraternity indicate that it "unquestionably shares much of the spirit of the present human rights movement," can also say that Islam "does not advance the basic idea of inalienable rights, nor does it avoid distinguishing according to sex and religion." In short, "Islamic theory does not present a notion of the rights of the individual. Rights do not attach to men qua men. It is more appropriate to refer to thc privileges of man."

It is plain enough that western culture is characterized by diverse perspectives on issues of human rights. Should one not expect a similar diversity within other world cultures and ideological frameworks? And how is one to evaluate this expectation without more extensive attention being paid to the statements of representatives of these cultures and ideologies? Any discussion of Islam and religious liberty must begin then with the stipulation that a dialogical approach requires a greater appreciation of the statements of Muslim on matters of human rights. Further, it is important to know the extent and nature of disagreement among representatives of Islam on these matters.

Our goal should be to understand the different perspectives that may be connected with the traditions of Islam. However, before we come to a discussion of these different perspectives in Islam and their approach towards human rights issues, it is important to lay out a little more fully the quality of attack which is made against Islam in general vis-a-vis, its attitude on the universal human rights issues. Pollis and Schwab conclude their essay "Human Rights: A Western Construct with Limited Applicability" by expressing a familiar objection to Euro-American ethnocentrism: "Unfortunately not only do human rights set forth in the universal declaration reveal a strong western bias, but there has been a tendency to view human rights a historically and in isolation from their social, political and economic milieu." This criticism is frequently applied to statements of rights that are contained in various internationally recognized human rights documents.

The complaint is that these are so many manifestations of a highly parochial cultural and historical experience in these statements that, at certain points, they neither have nor ought to have anything definitive, to say to peoples with other experience and traditions. The charge is a serious and challenging one. Human rights advocates need to face it squarely and respond to it with precision and care. The charges of western bias and cultural discrimination have been most persistently lodged by Muslims and by western students of Islam against the statements in various human right documents concerning the right to freedom of thought, conscience, and religion. Many of the Muslim objections were registered in 1948 during the deliberations that surrounded Article 18 of the Universal Declaration, which states:

> "Everyone has the right to freedom of thought, conscience and religion; this right includes the freedom to change his religion or belief, and freedom, 'either alone or in community with others in public or in private, to manifest his religion or belief in teaching, practice, worship and observance."

In response, a number of Islamic countries (in particular, Saudi Arabia) attempted to delete this article. Fading that, they blamed others - Lebanon, for example - for supporting it because, they contended, the rights of Lebanese Muslims would be compromised by such wording. Interestingly, the same attack could not be made on Pakistan, which also supported the article. Objections were raised by some of the same countries against the somewhat more elaborate version of the right to religious freedom contained in the draft of the International Covenant on Civil and Political Rights, which was later adopted and which stated:

> "No one shall be subject to coercion which would impair his freedom to have or to adopt a religion or belief of his choice (Article 18, sect. 2). And Article 26 of the covenant added another new stipulation which guaranteed equal protection of the law against any form of discrimination "on any ground such as race,... sex,... [or] religion."

Amazingly, more recently objections from much the same quarter were again raised in reaction to the draft of the Declaration on the Elimination of All Forms of

Intolerance and of Discrimination Based on Religion or Belief In spite of the fact that they did have some limited effect on the final version of the Declaration which was adopted by the UN General Assembly on 25th November, 1981, there was quite a reaction by Muslim political officials. There is also the question, in the wordings of sections 1 and 2 of Article 2 of the Declaration against Intolerance concerning legal discrimination "on grounds of religion and other belief - that is, of "any distinction, exclusion, restriction or preference based on religion or belief." In the light of these criticisms from Muslim quarters to the various statements cited above we must look at some of the historical and practical practices by Muslim states vis-a-vis the minorities residing in them. Even though, as is well known, non-Muslim monotheists (dhimmis) - namely Jews, Christians, Zoroastrians, and some others - are traditionally treated more tolerantly than polytheists and other kinds of "disbelievers," they were hardly accorded full and equal rights. So long as they lived peaceably they were allowed to practice their religion (in a subdued manner); but they were nevertheless required to pay a tax (jizya) to the Islamic state - described by Majid Khaddun "as a form of punishment of unbelief." What is more, Muslim a thorities at times prohibited the dhimmis from marrying Muslims and from conducting certain forms of business, and the dhimmis were required at times, according to traditional Islamic law, to wear distinctive clothing and to live in houses smaller than Muslim houses.

Finally, in certain Islamic states non-Muslims are prevented from occupying high public office, as, for example, in Pakistan and most Arab states where the head of state must be a Muslim. In short, the record shows that non-Muslims in Muslim countries do not enjoy the rights to life and liberty in the same measure as the Muslims. As Majid Khadduri put it,

> "As a subject of the Muslim state [the dhimmis suffered certain disabilities which reduced him to the status of a second-class citizen."

The conflict, then, seems clear. The articles on freedom of religion and conscience in various human rights documents appear to run a foul, at important points, of much "established" and "official' Muslim teaching about the treatment of apostates (murtads) and protected non-Muslims (dhimmis).

There are at least four possible strategies we might adopt in face of this conflict:

1. We might simply advocate retracting all statements in favour of freedom of religion and conscience (or we might accomplish the same purpose by rewriting existing statements so as to make them innocuous). There are problems with this response. Are all human rights statements to be retracted or emasculated whenever the encounter opposition? But, more to the point, there is actually little interest in the international community, even among Muslims, in taking such a radical step. Muslims, like others, seem committed to giving human rights status to freedom of religion and conscience, so long as those rights are properly restricted according to traditional teaching.
2. We might try to argue that devotion to existing freedom of religion statements entails allowing Muslim states, along with everyone else, discretion to define religious tolerance and its limits in

whatever way they see fit. We would then be allowing Muslims the right to follow their own consciences, and thus act on their internationally guaranteed right to religious liberty. There are two problems here. One is that tolerating all possible policies and views, even the most intolerant ones, yields a contradictory result, especially when intolerance toward certain beliefs can be enforced. Equally troublesome is the fact that existing statements of the rights to religious liberty explicitly include prohibitions that contradict certain Muslim policies and this may lead to reciprocal repression of Muslim minorities in non-Muslim states.

3. We might cling to existing statements of the right to religious liberty and attempt to enforce them internationally by means of the same devices that the United States, for example, has from time to time employed when trying to enforce other civil, political, and economic rights. There are no doubt special problems of feasibility in this case. Moreover, without agreeing that a belief in freedom of religion entails tolerating any belief, even those that enforce intolerance' it does seem that the cultural differences over this question create some subtleties and perplexities for human rights advocates that are not present in respect to the more notorious violations, such as gross mistreatment of prisoners, political opponents, etc.

4. We might use the contemporary debate between westerners and Muslims over freedom of religion and conscience as an occasion for reconsidering the foundations and character of a belief in such freedom both in the west and in the Islamic tradition. If, upon careful critical examination, the conflict

> between western and Islamic views concerning something 30 important and so basic a right to freedom of religion and conscience turns out to be much less clear and consistent and has been alleged, then we shall, I seems, have some reason to begin to call into question the "limited applicability" of human rights declarations.

Definitely, it is not difficult to show that Islam, like other of the world's religions, postulates a foundational division between two sorts of laws of behavior - "the Ways Of Allah" on the one hand, and "the ways of the world," on the other. The more sensitive question is whether the ways of Allah, after all, are systematically conceived in reference to a belief in the irreducible differentiation of the human person from "-worldly-causes and constraints. In other words, is there a law of the spirit, of the inner life, that from an Islamic point of view is sharply distinguished from the laws of the outer, including civil life. The answer is, affirmative, a verdict that has the most important consequences for understanding the idea of religious freedom in Islam. Just as there is evidence in the Qur'an that true religious belief is a deeply inward personal matter, a matter of the heart (kalb), there are firm grounds for several quite unexpected affirmations in the Qur'an of religious tolerance and forbearance. There is, to begin with, Sura 109, "The Unbelievers."

Presumably genuine submission or surrender to Allah's will, along with the appropriate dispositions of gratitude, devotion, steadfastness, etc., must come from the heart must involve and commitment. If that is true, then compulsion and external interference would appear to be the antithesis of Islamic faith.

As for those who divide their religion and break up

into sects, thou has no part in them in the least: Their affair is with Allah: he will in the end tell them the truth of all that they did (6:159: emphasis added).

If it had been thy Lord's Will, they would all have believed — all who were on earth! *Will thou then compel mankind, against their will, to believe!* (10:99 emphasis added).

Likewise did We make for every Messenger an enemy — evil ones among men and Jinns, inspiring each other with flowery discourses by way of deception. If thy Lord had so planned, they would not have done it: so leave them and their inventions alone (6:112).

The Qur'an leaves no doubt in these passages that it regards idolaters as profoundly in error. However, "their case will go to Allah." They are, it would appear, thereby excused from punishment, compulsion and other civil disabilities in relation to their religious beliefs and practices.

But how then shall we explain the obvious references in the Qur'an to the use of force in regard to idolaters and unbelievers? Some have argued that the message of the Qur'an is preoccupied with what might be called the political threat of religious unbelief. The Prophet's campaign to solidify and extend his political authority depended on religious as well as political loyalty form the contending factions, His struggle to subdue Medina and Mecca by creating an intricate confederation was wrought out of severe and constant struggles against these religio-political factions, and stability was constantly threatened by one or another of them.

These facts help explain the intensity of some Qur'anic utterances concerning disbelief and apostasy and the reasons for recommending the use of force in some cases against apostates.

A major area of disagreement between Islam and the human rights document is therefore freedom of religion. The Qur'an vigorously denounces those who renounce Islam for "the Devil has seduced them" away from the true faith. The major historical example is the revolt of the tribes after the death of the Prophet in A. D. 632. Abu Bakr, and jurists since then condemned secession from Islam (ridda) as doubly heinous : it is not only a violation of the compact of submission made with Allah, but it is also a breach of contract with his representatives on earth. It is, then, an offense both against God and against the state: it is both apostasy and treason. Par from having the right to become non-Muslim, the Muslim faces the death penalty as a sanction for such a charge. A careful review of the context in which such references occur, however, reveals that the only permissible use of force is defensive. That is, if non-Muslims themselves initiate the use of force for purpose of military conquest or religious persecution, or in breach of a solemn treaty, then and only then, it would appear, is forceful reaction justifiable. In other words, if this description is accurate, then the distinction as well as the symmetries between "morality" and "religion" are very much in play here. These passages justify force as retaliation for persecution and the threat of destruction. These are all presumably appeals to basic moral requirements either to keep promises and treaties, or to protect a community's basic welfare and security against aggression.

So construed, these injunctions to use force against unbelievers (and apostates) are grounded in emergency conditions, which consist of moral rather than religious provocation. That is, it is not primarily because the unbelievers hold the beliefs they do, but because of their manifest moral violations, that they are liable to punishment and coercion. At least, this account appears plausible, particularly because it provides a way to combine the strong emphasis on religious freedom in the Qur'an with the defense of compulsion against the apostates and others, also in the Qur'an. Thus the Qur'an's frequent justification for coercion and punishment against apostates and even unbelievers is in retaliation for breaking their agreement of covenant with the forces of the Prophet (and thus with Allah). In short, forceful countermeasures against an aggressive initiation of force are "morally" justified by conditions that are believed to bind all human beings, regardless of religious identity or affiliation. In this way we see that both the western and Islamic traditions share a common framework within which to think about freedom of conscience and religious liberty and many of the categories are mutually applicable in a most illuminating way.

So theologically we have to ask the question about the apparent paradox of the liberal spirit and over against it the statements in the Qur'an demanding the use of force in achieving one of the central ideals of Islamic revelation, the creation of a just social order. In his brilliant work on the Qur'an, Faxlur Rahman has shown that the aim of Islamic ideology, as it emerges from the Qur'an, is to create a just society, to "command good and forbid evil" (3.104, 110; 9.71). This would constitute a moral obligation "taken to be binding upon 'and available to all," and one to which "all people may be held accountable." Further, Rahman considers the implementation of Islamic theology as representing the social dimensions of taqwa, that is, keen moral perception and motivation. Rahman concludes that "with all its concern for a liberal pluralism for institutions and basic individual freedom, the Qur'an, under certain conditions, admits that the state, when representing society is paramount."

But at this point he forgets the essential- division of Islamic jurisprudence into ibadat (God-person relationship) and mu'amalat (person-person relationship) which does point to a sort of recognition of religious and interpersonal moral obligations, due to the complexity of the Qur'anic materials the distinction has not been conceptually worked out. This paper, it is hoped, has demonstrated the reasons for the deep tension in Islamic experience between a tolerant, pluralist spirit, on the one hand, and a more regimented, exclusivist stance on the other. Two general points, in closing are worth stressing.

First, in studying Islamic concepts, it is worthwhile to remember that in the linear progression of time characterized by historical process Islam developed as a religious phenomenon only after it was established as a political reality. Early political events and exigencies shaped the subsequent interpretation of Islamic ideology, often without regard for fairly obvious Qur'anic teaching. In the face of the expansion of Islamic political power and hegemony, the deep Qur'an impulse toward religious freedom steadily lost ground - in practice and in theory - to the equally strong concern for defending the faith against active persecution and violent assault. The defensive use of the force gradually gave way to more aggressive legal and political policies.

Second, the notions that underlie existing international human rights formulations in regard to freedom of religion and conscience are indeed relevant to cultures outside the west, including, it cannot be doubted, Islamic culture. There are without question, significant differences between the west and Islam in these matters. These are of course the result of a variety of dissimilar cultural and historical experiences. But there are also striking and revealing commonalities.

Further the theological and ethical implications of the Qur'anic teachings maintain the universality and objectivity of bask spiritual and moral truths, and hence shares the western understanding that in respect to matters of conscience all human beings are not only equal but equally accountable for any violations. It is, therefore, correct to conclude with confidence that there is much concurrence regarding the underlying commitments of Islam and the west to religious liberty.

Secularism

Basically, Religion constitutes an important element in the Indian culture. It has exercised a very significant influence in Indian civilisation. By becoming secular however India has not been anti-religious or irreligious. Rather she wants to be independent in her attitude towards all religions. Her age-old tradition of tolerance, magnanimity, free thinking and universal brotherhood has been amply reinforced by Constitutional provisions.

Dr. Rajendra Prasad, the first President of India, has made this position very clear by saying.

> "There are some who think that because we are a secular state, we do not believe in religious or spiritual values. Far from being so, it really means that in this country all are free to profess or preach the faith of their liking and that we wish well of all religions and want them to developed in their own way without any hindrance. India being a land of multi-religions, secularism is the

best arrangement ever made by any democratic country. Dr. B.R. Ambedkar explaining the concept "secular state" has remarked, "All that a secular state means is that this parliament shall not be competent to impose any particular religion upon the rest of the people".

Freedom of religion is fundamental to a secular State. That is, everybody can profess any religion. Imposition of any kind on religious ground is entirely forbidden. All citizens irrespective of their religious faith, will enjoy equality of rights. No religion community will be favoured or discriminated against and no instruction in religious dogma will be given in any public school. But it does not mean religious apathy or inertia. It rather promotes religious tolerance and equal reverence for all religions.

Thus by declaring India a secular state, the fathers of the Constitution have visualised fullest freedom, tolerance and liberal outlook in the most sentimental sensitive subject like religion. In a multi-religious society like India, it is desirable to make a distinction between "religious education" and "education about religions". The former means only the teaching of the principles and doctrines of a particular religion, whereas the latter is pertaining to a study of religion from a broad perspective. The Kothari Commission has aptly said the latter as "the eternal quest of the spirit". It is necessary for a multi-religious democratic state to promote a tolerant study of all religions, so that its citizens can understand each other better and live amicably together. It is however apprehended that since no instruction is given about any religion in schools, students will remain in dark about different religions. They will not have any idea about their own religion nor about others. The consequent general ignorance and misunderstanding about various religions may create conflict and tension among the citizens.

Webster's Dictionary says that "secularism" is the "belief that religion and ecclesiastical affairs should not enter into the functions of the State ..." A other alternative but negative definition given by Webster says, "A system of doctrines and practices that rejects any form of religious faith and worship". This emphasises a rational thinking about all religions and forms an important component of secularism. It is also logical to say that "a fair hearing of all points of view with special privileges accorded to none".

It has been rightly felt essential to develop a more secular outlook amongst those who profess various religions. It would be possible according to some thinkers by an adequate study of science with its stress on open mindedness tolerance and objectivity.

It is also argued that there should not be any watertight compartments between spiritual and secular matters. Because spiritual matters have secular roots and secular matters have spiritual roots. In the words of Dr. Iqbal.

> "the spirit finds its opportunity in the materials, the natural and secular. All that is secular is, therefore, sacred in the roots of its being".

This should work as a guidance for our future development in the direction. Both science and spirit should go hand in hand. The scientific eventual emergence of a society which would promote the development of the whole well-integrated man, not the fragmented and unbalanced personality.

Education in the Independent India comes under the State control and is quite secular and non-denominational, children as future citizen must get that education which should aim at their development irrespective of religious affiliation or social status. They are to be taken as citizens not as members of this or that religious group. India should be released from her past religious traditions and pursue the path of free religious activities in a secular manner. As has been said earlier, secularism does not mean that religions should be banished from the educational scene and rather both should be well-integrated in a process which is dynamic and conducive to change and progress.

Secular education should be taken as a quest for knowledge and spirit in an objective and tolerant manner, not as a conquest of faith and religious ideas embedded in our culture. It should aim at questions, rather than answers to religious pursuits. True secular education must be built in individuals' potentiality and eternal quests, not blind faith and biased, attitudes. It must be based on morality, justice, free thinking and service. As far as religious instruction is concerned, the entire advocational system may be divided into three categories:

(i) Government,

(ii) Aided, and

(iii) Purely private or special.

Government institutions are solely maintained out of public funds and as per the Constitutional provisions under Art. 281 no religious instruction can be imparted in these schools and colleges. The aided institutions are taken as semi-government and as such the management may make arrangements for religious instruction without effecting anybody's sentiment. Government can neither favour nor disfavour such religious education in educational institutions. The purely private organisations are set up by religious or other endowments. These institutions do not receive any assistance from government and are free to import any religious instructions without any interference from government.

Secularism in education theoretically may be interpreted as religions mentality of education. In practice however all religions are excluded from the curriculum and no instruction on any religion is imparted in schools and colleges. Such principle of neutrality holds good in the normal/formal educational system. But to any discerning eye it will be visible that a large majority of our schools are not really neutral to religions. Religious creeps into educational process in different ways stealthly and unassumingly. It comes through morning prayers, staging mythological plays, celebrating festivals, decorating classrooms and so on.

Even teachers impart religious instruction unconsciously as their talks, discussion and clarification in classrooms have religious overtones and express their religious faiths and mores. Therefore, it is called that in every country a "Hidden curriculum" works in disguise and the religions of the dominant group in the locality gradually influences the programmes in educational institutions. This is not peculiar to India only, it is a fact even in all advanced countries like USA, UK, etc. Therefore utmost attempts should be made to plug these loops so that there cannot be any infiltration of religious bigotry or denominational ideas. A secular culture based on rational outlook should emerge in this country which will encourage tolerance, free thinking and receptivity among students. The good elements of all religions should be taught to them and great savants as well as saints of different religions who sacrificed their lives for the cause of the national/social well being should be made known to all. Religious neutrality or secularity is a matter of attitude which can be developed in students by living and learning by experiencing and realising the truths of religions.

The programmes both curricular and co-curricular should be organised in such a way that students can have positive and unbiased attitude towards all religions. This is necessary not only for success of democracy, but also for national integration. Development of attitudes can be possible not merely by teaching of suitable topics or subjects, but by inculcating the desirable values and sentiments through real participation and experiences. Teachers should work as living models or ideals whose objective attitude and unbiased activities can be emulated by their students. This is more necessary when the society is threatened by narrow bigotry, religious fanaticism and blind superstitions. Originally the Constitution of India did not have the word "Secular" explicitly.

But it was implicit in the sense that we cannot have real democracy in a pluralistic society without secularism. Equality is ensured by Secularism and Secularism is guaranteed by equality which is available only in the true democracy. But it was realised that mere implication of secularism from the Constitutional provisions might not be enough. It should be specifically and explicitly mentioned in the Preamble. Hence in the 42nd Amendment of the Constitution, the term "Secular" was added. But recently the Communal venom has been infused into the body politic of the country by some political parties and persons with vested interests to take undue advantage at the polls or in elections.

In his broadcast to the nation on December 6, 1992 on the Babri-Masjid Ayodhya issue, Sri P.V. Narasimha Rao, Prime Minister of India has aptly said,

> "In a country of the size and diversity like ours, it is only the concern and care of the sensibilities of each other which can ensure a smooth functioning of the institutions that we have created. This is the only way to maintain peace and harmony amongst the people of India. Whatever may be our differences on political, social and economic issues they have to be acted upon keeping this wider concept in view. The delicate fabric of our nation woven around democracy and secularism is the Only anchor-sheet for our country's existence".

Promotion of human rights can be possible only through democratic and secular living based on appropriate rights and duties of citizens.

Mutually Exclusive or Supportive

The 1948 Universal Declaration of Human Rights (UDHR) makes no mention of religion as a possible basis for such fundamental rights. Although there was an attempt by the Dutch delegate Father De Beaufort OP to amend the preamble with a reference to "Man's divine origin and his eternal destiny," this was rejected as being contrary to the universal nature of the declaration. For the Saudi Arabian delegate, the fact that the declaration began and ended with the human being, without any reference to God, was sufficient reason to abstain.

Indeed, Father Beaufort's formula would have been rather out of place. The Universal Declaration stems from a secular religion (religion in the classical sense of 'binding'), which arose from two centuries of Enlightenment thinking. Its starting point lies in the fundamental freedoms of the individual which have to be protected against the power of the Sovereign (the State). Although the text does refer in the final articles to the community and duties of individuals with respect to the community, the gist of the UDHR remains centred on the individual. In the period following the adoption of the Declaration the human rights project was interpreted as a juridical challenge to legislate and to create procedural provisions for judgment of individual and state complaints. On the basis of an intrinsically neutral attitude towards the culture, regime and level of prosperity in the country concerned, human rights violations would have to be denounced everywhere.

Indeed, generalised statements on the superiority of human rights to religion can provoke violent reactions, as UN observer Bilo experienced in Sudan. His remark on the subservience of the Qur'an to human rights provided the Sudanese government with an excellent opportunity to switch from a defensive to an offensive position. Despite attempts to promote the human rights project as some sort of civil religion, its moral foundations remain subject to continuous discussion. Besides objections to ideas that would seem to put the human being above God, there are also religious endorsements of human rights of an unrestrictive nature. Such positive statements are based upon the view that human rights in essence are God-given. Thus, in 1992 the Latin American bishops endorsed the human rights concept as follows:

> The equality of all human beings, created as they are in the image of God, is guaranteed and completed in Christ. From the time of his incarnation, when the Word assumes our nature and especially through his redemption on the cross, He demonstrates the value of every single human being. Therefore Christ, God and man,

> constitutes also the deepest source and guarantee for the dignity of the human person. Each violation of human rights is contrary to God's plan.

The gospel is thus seen as the deepest foundation of all human rights. These rights, however, are grossly and systematically violated from day to day "not only by terrorism, repression and attacks ... but also through the existence of extreme poverty and unjust economic structures which result in extreme inequality. Political intolerance and indifference in regard to the situation of general impoverishment reveal a general contempt for concrete human life on which we cannot remain silent." Hence, as a "pastoral action line" the bishops requested the promotion of human rights in an effective and courageous manner "based on both the gospel and the social doctrine of the Church, by word, action and cooperation, and in that way to commit ourselves to the defence of the individual and social rights of human beings, peoples, cultures and marginalised sectors of society, together with persons in a state of extreme vulnerability and prisoners."

Now we come to some very crucial issues.

Does Religion Need Human Rights?

In fact, Religion provides people with a transcendental basis for morally justified behaviour. From a reality beyond direct human experience moral standards are set which cannot be altered. Does this mean that respect for human rights is inherent in all religion? Practice shows it does not. First, the religious message itself may contain inhuman elements. This applies particularly to situations in which, apart from the religious core of the message its cultural setting; too is authorised and absolutised.

Religion may then sanctify a whole people or caste and hence will come into conflict with the principle of human equality Generally, such faith is based on tradition and interpretation rather than the holy scriptures themselves. Besides fossilisation of a certain cultural context from the past, contemporary religion, too, may be subject to socio-political manipulation. Thus, after the Rwandan genocide Justin Hakizimana, an elder in the Presbyterian Church, observed that the church and the government had become too close: The church went hand in hand with the politics of Habyarimana. We did not condemn what was going on because we were corrupted. None of our churches, especially the Catholics, has condemned the massacres. That is why all the church leaders have fled, because they believe they may be in trouble with their own people.

The corruption of religious institutions is a gradual process which may strongly embarrass people retrospectively. This is strikingly expressed in the reaction of Reverend Mugamera, who lost his whole family (his wife and six children) in the Rwandan bloodshed: Who would deny a crucial role to human rights in that new start for religion in Rwaada? Indeed, religion per se appeared to be insufficiently equipped to deal with the politically inspired processes of exclusion (us, not them!), thinking of others as enemies, demonisation and final extermination. The abuse of power is as old as human history. Therefore power should always be bound, i.e., tied to certain norms. Where such norms express the fundamental freedoms and entitlements of each and every human being, we speak of 'human rights'. These are prima facie rights that are supposed to trump all other types of claims, both private and public. This applies to religious power too. Religion is subject to both ideologisation and institutionalisation.

Human rights, on the contrary, put the human being above ideology and the dignity of the individual person above the organisation.

Religion needs human rights — including the fundamental freedom to criticise the use of power. The new High Commissioner of the United Nations for Human Rights attached an immediate priority to Rwanda. Training programmes for human rights monitors started everywhere in that country. Would this achieve better protection against ethnicism, discrimination and genocide than the teaching of the churches could apparently offer? A sceptical undertone is detectable already in the question itself.

The global human rights project possesses its own institutions: inter-governmental and non-governmental centres, complaints procedures with commissions, committees and courts of law, training programmes and academic teaching courses. Human rights are already seen as a "global religion" and that is meant in an institutional sense as well.

Do Human Rights Need Religion?

Human rights have been authoritatively defined in the Universal Declaration of Human Rights, based on a morally forceful rhetoric. The articles specifying the various rights all begin with the word everyone. Everyone counts. However the declaration may have been drafted — "written in two days in a hotel room in San Francisco by Eleanor Roosevelt and two assistants" it is a simple fact that these words have a universal appeal. While this may not be the case in regard to all rulers, it certainly does apply to the ruled. Just like holy scriptures such as the Bible, the Qur'an and the Bhagavad Gita, the UDHM appeals to a much wider circle of people than the cultural context in which it originated.'

Anyone who has ever carried a copy of the Universal Declaration in its pocket in countries with tyrannical regimes knows that, in a cultural context entirely different from the West, there can be an overwhelming demand for this document. Although the history of civil and political rights is tuned in particular to the protection of citizens against sovereigns who want to rob them of their possessions in a Third World context the Declaration functions as a basis for the emancipation of the have-nots. The Universal Declaration is generally considered to be positive law (international customary law). It was followed by numerous international covenants, conventions, protocols and declarations of the General Assembly of the United Nations. Although in a legal sense their universality is now almost undisputed and a great deal of political consensus on the human rights idea exists as well, there are still serious difficulties in implementing human rights.

Obviously, the inclusion of these rights in legal texts is in itself insufficient. It is often precisely in states with the most serious human rights violations that we find the most beautiful constitutional clauses on fundamental freedoms and entitlements. Accessible procedures of a supra-national nature have been effectively created only in Europe. But in order to bring a case before the European Court of Justice all local remedies have to be exhausted. This may take a long time and it may also require a considerable investment in lawyers' fees. Contentious action, however important as a remedy for human rights violations, has to be, accompanied by socio-cultural and political action aiming at the inculturation of human rights.

To have a right does not automatically imply that all reasonable claims based on it will be realised. Rights in general and human rights in particular tend to be more action-oriented. The real question is not the universality of the human rights idea itself but a universal reception of that idea.

No single culture in the sense of a way of life transferred from one generation to the next is fully receptive to the notion of universal human dignity and equality. It is an illusion to think that this idea might be simply disseminated by means of readable material.

In some Western countries, liberal policies on pornography are legally regarded as a consequence of the basic freedom of expression (freedom of the press. Such a view illustrates well the contingency of human rights as a secular religion connected to a universalist legal System with clearly defined procedures and institutions. There is no way to escape the necessity of weighing one person's freedom to express against another person's freedom to regard certain expressions as dehumanising, repugnant and hence intolerable. There are, indeed, certain reasons can be adduced for the decriminalisation of the production, distribution and consumption of pornography, but human rights is definitely not one of them. It is precisely such ways of reasoning that are used elsewhere to construe human rights as not universal at all but rather as a caricature of Western thinking.

Peeping through the jurisprudence of the European, Court of Human Rights reveals a surprisingly large number of cases in which criminal suspects and convicted persons invoke certain articles in the European Convention for the Protection of Human Rights and Fundamental Freedoms (Rome Treaty of 1950) in regard to criminal procedure. This is not unimportant- the protection of everyone against the abuse of power, including criminals, constitutes the core of human rights. Yet it is clearly not the jurisprudence of the European Court in Strassbourg that is going to provide the human rights project with the necessary cultural roots.

Remarkably, the main challenge is the implementation of the right to life and to a dignified human existence in daily life. The Human Rights project bases this upon the notion of universal responsibility. In our global village that responsibility is being taken up so poorly that the project itself has already lost much credibility. The acceptance of responsibility requires more than just a legal basis, no matter how universal that foundation may be. Indeed, the ratification of treaties, the establishment of courts of human rights and the development of a human rights jurisprudence is not enough. The moral grounds for a conviction upon which responsible behaviour rests have to be constantly nurtured on the basis of a world view. In so far as the notion of human rights finds its origin in individualism, it is responsible individualism that obtains. This is evidently not the same as possessive individualism. Yet the former may easily degenerate into the latter.

It is exactly those cultures in which possessive individualism has strong roots — and that includes the global village as such - that experience great difficulty with economic and social rights, already at the stage of standard-setting. While individualism may offer a sufficient moral foundation for respecting everyone's fundamental freedoms, it is inadequate as a basis for accepting other people's needs as grounds for justified claims. Economic, social and cultural rights presuppose not just free individuals but a community that accepts responsibility for the fulfilment of everybody's basic needs. The liberal-democratic idea [according to Fukuyama, the end of the history of ideas fails here. "The strong", as the Greek historian Thucydides put it, "do what is in their power while the weak accept their fate." In the free market economy the weak find no structural protection against unemployment, disease, disability, and old age. For good reasons, dependence on the charity of the strong was considered unsatisfactory. In many industrialised countries measures such as workers' protection, compulsory education, professional training, and health protection constituted a structural attempt towards the realisation of economic and social rights. The social struggle that led to such achievements was nurtured by religion in the sense of a set of ideas transcending individual existence.

Friedrich Hayek, the godfather of neo-liberalism, once wrote a book under the title *The Mirage of Social justice.* It is only a negative notion of freedom, he feels (keep your hands off other people's property, allow everyone her liberty) that can be more than a mirage. Hence, for a vision of social justice we have to look elsewhere. John Rawls is well known as a philosopher who has attempted to construct political principles of justice applicable to any society that tackles the problem of inequalities among people as well. His "non-normative" theory is based on a hypothetical social contract between citizens who, behind a "veil of ignorance" regarding their relative success or failure in acquiring entitlement positions, decide what is socially "fair." This is not the place to review that theory critically, but what is noteworthy is that Rawls's rational-liberal theory of justice failed him when he tried to construct a political law of peoples that would legitimate human rights on the basis of reason only. For one thing, he feels compelled to abandon the three egalitarian features of his theory of justice: the fair value of political liberties, fair equality of opportunity and the difference principle.

Thus, his human rights concept deals only with civil rights and excludes political and socio-economic rights. His argument then implies that even representatives of hierarchical societies, committed in a rather absolute sense to certain ideologies and religions, placed behind a veil of ignorance (the basic assumption in hypothetical contract theory) would accept the same "law of peoples," including; basic civil rights, as democratic societies. But why would they? As Stanley Hoffmann puts it:

Are societies whose governments are dogmatically committed to ideology or religion likely to respect basic human rights at all? Since there are no free elections, how would we know that their "system of law" meets "the essentials of legitimacy in the eyes of [their] own people"? Whatever the answer, what is clear is that Rawls's law of peoples has been shaped so as to appeal to a purely hypothetical group of peoples.

The fallacy here is in the parallel Rawls seems to draw between an "overlapping consensus" of comprehensive doctrines that endorse a single conception of justice within a democratic political culture..., and an "overlapping consensus" of societies based on very different political conceptions of justice. Such different societies could only endorse a very weak -law of peoples." (Hoffmann, 1995, 54).

Hence, for a stronger "law of peoples" we have to look beyond non-ideal theory" (Rawls). Indeed, we cannot escape the search in the conceptual roots of human rights within the various religious themselves. Research done by Wronka, would point to a preliminary conclusion that the idea of one person's responsibility for satisfaction of another person's needs is common to all world religions (Wronka, 1992).

One example is the Old Testament term d-q-h, which implies the acknowledgement of the claims of the poor, purely on basis of their need.

Thus, the connection with religion may provide the all sorts of political and economic constraints to the implementation of human rights, there also exists a major obstacle in the cultural resistance to norms and values implying that people are responsible for the well-being of their fellow human beings. A culture of contentment predominates in the post-Cold War era, paralysing the global 'haves'. Christopher Lasch speaks of a rebellion of the elites and the betrayal of democracy (Lasch, 1994). With so many people excluded from a decent existence, the human rights project suffers from structural day-to-day violation.

It is noteworthy that in the processes of ideologisation and institutionalisation, religion continually loses credibility. To ensure that religiously 'sanctified ends cannot justify any means, human rights have to be respected in church and mosque too. At the same time, the global project for universal responsibility of people for one another's freedom and welfare cannot do without constant moral injection. It is primarily in, their transcendental orientation that human beings learn to rise above their immediate patterns of needs. Similarly, it is in down-to-earth challenges to satisfy human needs that religion attains concrete relevance.

In its relation to society religion has a dual character. It is precisely because religion transcends the daily concerns of the individual that it has to meet higher demands of credibility. Doubtless, a lack of social credibility is one of the factors which makes a revitalisation of religion imperative. Here, more is at stake than Auschwitz and

Rwanda, notwithstanding the horrific nature of such human catastrophes.

Christianity could not prevent slavery and colonialism; in an institutional sense it has even been part of many forms of human exploitation. Indeed, the rights of human beings to food, clothing, shelter, education, health, employment and a decent standard of living are still being violated from day to day. In many respects the systematic contravention of economic and social rights is related to global monetary and financial structures, "edifices of sin" as Pope John Paul II called them in his encyclical Solicitude rei socialis. A quick glance at the map of world religions today reveals that it is Christians in particular who benefit from such structures.

As long as the global maintenance of basic human rights is not regarded as a real concern in the 'Christian' West, the Christian religion will continue to suffer from a fundamental lack of credibility.

To conclude, it may be safely surmised that all religons of world have clear directions for mutual tolerance, social/ communal harmony, thus maintaining the righteousness and social justice and protection of human rights.

REFERENCES

Brian Kemble Pennington *Was Hinduism Invented?* New York: Oxford University Press US, 2005.

Daniel Dubuisson. *The Western Construction of Religion*. 1998. William Sayers (trans.) Baltimore: Johns Hopkins University Press, 2003. p. 90.

George A. Lindbeck, *Nature of Doctrine* (Louisville: Westminster/ John Knox Press, 1984), 33.

Isomae Jun'ichi. "Deconstructing 'Japanese Religion'". *Japanese Journal of Religious Studies* 32.2: 235–248.

Jason Ânanda Josephson. "When Buddhism Became a 'Religion'". *Japanese Journal of Religious Studies* 33.1: 143–168.

S.N. Balagangadhara. *The Heathen in His Blindness...* New York: Brill Academic Publishers, 1994. p.159.

Talal Asad, *Genealogies of Religion*. Baltimore: Johns Hopkins Univ. Press, 1993 p.34-35.

Timothy Fitzgerald. *Discourse on Civility and Barbarity.* Oxford University Press, 2007. pp. 45-46.

Bibliography

Ahmed, Mufti Md. M. (2006). *Rights and Liberties under Islam,* Anmol, New Delhi,

Ankerl, Guy (2000). *Global Communication without Universal Civilization, vol.1: Coexisting contemporary civilizations: Arabo-Muslim, Bharati, Chinese, and Western.* INU societal research. Geneva: INU Press.

Arnold, Matthew (1869). *Culture and Anarchy.* New York: Macmillan. Third edition, 1882, available online. Retrieved: 2006-06-28.

Bakhtin, M.M. (1981). *The Dialogic Imagination: Four Essays.* Ed. Michael Holquist. Trans. Caryl Press.

Balagangadhara, S.N. (1994). *The Heathen in His Blindness...* New York: Brill Academic Publishers.

Barua, Jyanti (2001). *Social Mobilisation and Modern Society,* Mittal, New Delhi.

Barzilai, Gad. (2003). *Communities and Law: Politics and Cultures of Legal Identities* University of Michigan Press.

Bhabha, Jacqueline (1996). "Embodied Rights: Gender Persecution, State Sovereignty, and Refugees." *Public Culture,* 9:3-32.

Binion, Gayle (1995). "Human Rights: A Feminist Perspective." *Human Rights Quarterly,* 17:509-526.

Bourdieu, Pierre. (1977). *Outline of a Theory of Practice.* Cambridge University Press.

Brian Kemble Pennington (2005). *Was Hinduism Invented?* New York: Oxford University Press US.

Chandra, Ashish (2000). *Human Rights and Conflict Resolution,* Rajat, New Delhi.

Cohen, Anthony P. (1985). *The Symbolic Construction of Community.* Routledge: New York.

Cook, Rebecca (1994). *Human Rights of Women. National and International Perspectives.* University of Pennsylvania Press, Philadelphia.

Daniel Dubuisson (2003). *The Western Construction of Religion.* 1998. William Sayers (trans.) Baltimore: Johns Hopkins University Press.

Dawkiins, R. (1982). *The Extended Phenotype: The Long Reach of the Gene.* Paperback ed., 1999. Oxford Paperbacks.

Findley & Rothney (1986). *Twentieth-Century World* Houghton Mifflin.

Forsberg, A. *Definitions of culture* CCSF Cultural Geography course notes. Retrieved: 2006-06-29.

Geertz, Clifford. (1973). *The Interpretation of Cultures: Selected Essays.* New York.

George A. Lindbeck (1984). *Nature of Doctrine* (Louisville: Westminster/John Knox Press.

Goodall, J. (1986). *The Chimpanzees of Gombe: Patterns of Behavior.* Cambridge, MA: Belknap Press of Harvard University Press.

Gupta, N.L. (2002). *Human Values for the 21st Century,* Anmol, New Delhi.

Hoult, T.F., ed. (1969). *Dictionary of Modern Sociology.* Totowa, New Jersey, United States: Littlefield, Adams & Co.

Isomae Jun'ichi. "Deconstructing 'Japanese Religion'". *Japanese Journal of Religious Studies* 32.2: 235–248.

Jary, D. and J. Jary. (1991). *The HarperCollins Dictionary of Sociology*. New York: HarperCollins.

Jason Ânanda Josephson. "When Buddhism Became a 'Religion'". *Japanese Journal of Religious Studies* 33.1: 143–168.

Kanitkar, Satish (2000). *International Provision of Human Rights*, Rajat, New Delhi.

Pandit Madhusudan (2009). *Fundamental Human Rights: What, Why & Where,* Swastik, Delhi.

Peters, Julie and Andrea Wolper (1995). *Women's Rights, Human rights. International Feminist Perspectives.* Routledge, NY.

Rao, Arati (1995). *The Politics of Gender and Culture in International Human Rights Discourse.* in Peters and Wolper ed. (1995).

Sachdeva Mann, Harveen (1995). Women's Rights Versus Feminism? Postcolonial Perspectives. *Postcolonial Discourse and Changing Cultural Contexts.* Gita Rajan and Radhika Mohanram, eds. Greenwood Press, Westport, CN.

Shah Giriraj et al. (2005). *Human Rights: Free and Equal,* Anmol, New Delhi.

Talal Asad, *Genealogies of Religion*. Baltimore: Johns Hopkins Univ. Press, 1993 p.34-35.

Timothy Fitzgerald (2007). *Discourse on Civility and Barbarity.* Oxford University Press.

Yadav, J.P. (2004). *Human Rights and Social Security,* Anmol, New Delhi.

Index

■■■